MW00441519

Never forget 9/11
Capt. Al Fuentes

American By Choice

By

Captain Alfredo Fuentes, F.D.N.Y.
with
Donald MacLaren and Helen Morrissey Rizzuto

Embrace Life & American

Fire Dreams Publishing Co.
P.O. Box 98
Island Park, NY 11558

www.atlasbooks.com
1-800-247-6553

International Standard Book Number 0-9753168-0-X
Library of Congress Control Number: 2004102850

Dedicated to my parents Alfredo & Aida

Because of their vision, struggle and dedication,
I was able to begin my journey as an

American by Choice

CONTENTS

PART ONE – BEGINNINGS

PART TWO
SEPTEMBER 11TH, 2001 – EILEEN FUENTES

PART THREE – RECOVERY AND BEYOND

PART FOUR – EYEWITNESS ACCOUNTS

Lazarus

They don't tell us in the Bible
About Lazarus after
Jesus called him out
They don't tell us
If he ever shared the secret
Of that tomb before
They pulled away
The stone

We don't know if the taste of dust
Ever left his throat completely, or if he ever awakened
In the dark night-blooming jasmine air and wondered
At the paleness of the moon

We don't learn anything at all
But once, I walked home with them
Along that road to Mary and Martha's
In the bright afternoon sun
After they had wiped their tears
And rubbed their sore hands free of rock soil

One Sunday in those days when clerics
Would go on with the mass in Latin
I stayed behind, taking my time
Listening to the quiet
Laughter, watching them each turn around
And see him as if for the first time

How they luxuriated in their love
And forgot for a little while
About the worrisome things
Like sickness and death and paying the bills

(for Captain Alfredo Fuentes, F.D.N.Y.,
his rescuers and family)

Helen Morrissey Rizzuto
from *Under The Hell Gate*

NOTE

American by Choice is divided into four distinct
parts: Beginnings; September 11, 2001 –; Recovery and
Beyond, and Eyewitness Accounts. It should be noted
that the point of view is not the same throughout the
book. Part One, Beginnings, is in my voice, but because
of the injuries I suffered in the attack on the World Trade
Center on the morning of September 11, 2001, and the
medically induced coma that followed, my wife Eileen
picks up the story and is the narrator of Part II.
Interwoven are three pieces by my children, Matthew,
Caitlin and Elizabeth. Part III, Recovery and Beyond, is
in my voice, and Part IV, Eyewitness Accounts, is in the
voice of my rescuers.

PART ONE
BEGINNINGS

CHAPTER ONE

SEPTEMBER 11TH, 2001

September 11th, 2001 started out as one of those beautiful days you wished would last forever – low humidity, clear blue sky, bright sunshine – but it would soon be marked with dread. The events of the next few hours were about to change my life and career forever.

Unlike the way I feel on days when I'm faced with bad weather and traffic problems, I felt relaxed on the fifty-five minute drive from my home in Long Beach, Long Island to the Brooklyn Navy Yard. I started on the road as usual, at around 5:30 a.m. and drove along the Belt Parkway that passes Coney Island and overlooks the Atlantic Ocean, where a bright yellow sun was just rising above the horizon. The only thing missing was the ringing of church bells to start the day. I pulled my Battalion Chief's car into the parking lot of the New York City Fire Department's Marine Division, located inside the historic Brooklyn Navy Yard on the East River at 6:30 to start my tour at 0700.

The F.D.N.Y. Marine Division is the headquarters for the fireboats that protect the greater New York Harbor.

Firefighters who like the water tend to gravitate to this division. The fireboat companies are a twenty-four hour operation and have the same tours as the land companies: 9 a.m. to 6 p.m. and 6 p.m. to 9 a.m.; however, I was always on call twenty-four hours, should a need arise.

After having been in the F.D.N.Y. for twenty-five years, and after having worked in many busy firehouses, including two Rescue companies, I had been asked by Chief of the Fire Department and friend, Pete Ganci, if I would be the Acting Battalion Chief of the Marine Division, while a search was conducted for a chief with a marine background.

This new assignment put me in charge of the 560 miles of harbor shoreline and any fires and related emergencies in the New York City Harbor.

A rich tradition exists in the Marine Division, with many of the fireboats respectfully named in memory of deceased firefighters who died in the line of duty: Marine Co.#6's fireboat is named "The Kevin Kane," while Marine Co #1, located on the west side of Manhattan on the Hudson River has "The McKean," and Marine Co. #9's in Staten Island is "The Firefighter," a name that brings music to my ears.

Since 9/11 came on a workday, and after the Labor Day weekend that signals the official end of the summer season, I expected fewer pleasure boats to be in the harbor, making it less likely to have many rescue calls on such a beautiful day. If we were called out, it would probably be to help a minor boat in distress or to recover a jumper. Kathleen, my secretary, would be coming in an hour later at 0800 hours, so I began my usual routine of making a pot of coffee and checking on what was happening, including the day's activities planned for all the fireboats, including Marine Co. 6, which shared our quarters along the East River.

My office had a picture window that looked out on a beautiful view of the lower Manhattan skyline, with the imposing World Trade Center rising above it. With a cup of coffee in hand, I settled in at my desk, to begin my daily paperwork. Kathleen and the others started coming in, and everyone commented on the beautiful day.

Shortly after we'd all begun our work, I became aware of a change in the atmosphere in the office; strange things were happening: Kathleen had begun to talk in a loud voice, which was unusual for her, and people started running past the door. Suddenly, Kathleen ran into my office, a frightened look on her face, and said, "Cap, a plane just hit the World Trade Center!"

What is there to say when you're told the unimaginable? It was a clear day. How could a pilot hit the Trade Center on a clear day?

"It hit the World Trade Center," she repeated.

I jumped up to follow her over to our window. I'd always felt I could almost touch those buildings, if I just reached out. Other staff members had already gathered to see the unbelievable. "Oh my God," they were saying; when I looked, I couldn't believe my own eyes. The North Tower, or Tower One, had its upper section engulfed in fire and smoke. I immediately started sizing up the situation − six to eight floors with heavy fire, volumes of black smoke, heavy structural damage to the top section of the high-rise tower, the building's mechanical and infrastructure damaged, and thousands of people trapped above. I could see a major part of the building's façade had a large rupture created by the impact of the fast-moving, angled plane. The unimaginable was now real.

I had to devise a plan that would put the fireboats into action immediately. We were going to have hundreds dead, thousands possibly. I would surround the tip of lower Manhattan and the Battery Park area with the fireboats, because the West Side Highway and F.D.R. Drive would probably be impassable. The fireboats could be used to supply and relay river water to augment the water supply for the land units operating at the World Trade Center, and they could transport the injured to waiting ambulances in the surrounding boroughs of Brooklyn and Queens.

"If we have to, we'll arrange loading areas in Brooklyn, Queens and Staten Island to pick up and transport firefighters to the World Trade Center. Prepare for possible pick-up sites of the land units," I advised everyone.

As my staff started responding to my orders, I called the Manhattan dispatcher and said, "This is Captain Fuentes, Marine Division. Have my fireboats respond to the Battery Park area, except Marine 9." I wanted Marine 9 available to respond to any other emergency that might arise in the harbor.

"The Kevin Kane," Marine Co.6's fireboat, was scheduled to have maintenance work done to it, so we had "The Smoke" as a replacement fireboat for Marine 6 that day. I radioed Marine Co.1 to respond to lower Manhattan on the West side, but they had responded initially and assigned on the box: M-55-8057. A fifth alarm was initially transmitted on the box for the fire. I quickly grabbed my gear and started out to board the boat that I had ordered to Battery Park in Lower Manhattan, and the West side.

That was my game plan, to surround lower Manhattan with our fireboats, so that they'd be ready to be put into action. Our fireboats can get in close to the Manhattan shoreline because the pilots and officers are experienced. There are depth gauges to guide them, but the pilots and officers know the waters well, their depths, their currents and their best places to berth. I knew I'd be getting off Marine 6 when we berthed, because it was my job to notify the chiefs at the

Command Post that I had surrounded the Battery Park area with the fireboats.

Just before leaving my office, there was something I remembered from the 1993 bombing of the World Trade Center, when I assisted in that attack. On that day, the firefighters' radio communications were a problem, and the F.D.N.Y. still had not improved the firefighters' radios for those high-rise communications. I had told my men during drills at Brooklyn's Rescue Company 2, "Any time you go into these high-rise buildings for emergencies or for a fire, the handy talkies are going to be a pain in the neck. They're not going to operate properly. The officers should take the portable citywide radio, in order to communicate directly to the dispatcher, in case of immediate danger and need for assistance." The radio I referred to we'd named the "super" radio. It has the same frequencies found on the fire apparatus, and with a simple flip of the switch, I had the option of using it as a handy-talkie or as a means of communicating with all five boroughs directly, through the dispatchers. I reminded myself to take my super radio, because I'd need to talk directly to the dispatchers.

Marine 1 was already responding, when I hopped on Marine 6. I kept sizing up the scene and thinking about what more we could do as we made our way down the East River. By the time we passed underneath the Brooklyn Bridge and came to the tip of Battery Park, my pilot Bill Hannan, and spare pilot Ed Mauro, with whom I had worked in both Rescue 1 and 2, decided to berth at the North Cove Marina on the Hudson River, on the West side of Manhattan. That would put me conveniently about three blocks from the World Trade Center and the Command Post.

As we neared Battery Park, billowing smoke poured out of the burning North Tower, and desperate people were starting to jump out the windows. The heat in such an inferno, fueled by jet fuel, would rise above thousands of degrees, giving them only two horrific choices of death.

Suddenly, I looked up and saw a commercial airliner heading south, down the Hudson River. God, that plane's low, I remember thinking. It passed directly over us, and to my amazement, whoever was piloting banked the jet to the left. As it turned and headed north, I thought, oh God, no; then I heard the engines roaring faster. He had deliberately accelerated. The jet roared directly overhead; all of us on the fireboat were looking up; we had all seen him bank the plane's wings, just before impact. I'm convinced, even now, that his plan was to take out more floors.

The jet crashed into the South tower with a horrific, thunderous, deafening sound, followed by the eruption of a giant orange fireball. It was a sight I might expect to see in a movie, but never in real life. I still get chills remembering it. The fireball rose to a height that reached past the roof of the tower. I never saw the plane come out on the other side.

My entire crew and I were stunned. "We're at war," I said to one of my firefighters on my left. Not only had we witnessed a deliberate attack on one of the World Trade Towers, we were now faced with two of the worst high-rise fires I had ever seen. On the way to the marina, I had just about convinced myself that Tower One must have been some kind of freak accident, but the second plane turned my stomach. I knew we wouldn't be able to extinguish fires that were burning out of control some eighty and more floors up, with an open individual floor area of approximately 40,000 square feet per floor. I could only imagine the structural damage to the exterior and the interior of the buildings and to the mechanical systems on multiple floors. The primary objective would be to evacuate and save as many lives as possible.

As firefighters, we're trained to fight fires and to save lives. As I observed the two burning towers from Marine 6, I began to think that we might have as many as 10,000 people trapped above the impact zones. It would be a Herculean task to get our firefighters up eighty and more floors in order to start the evacuations and rescues. I was about to become involved in a rescue attempt like no other I had ever been in before.

CHAPTER TWO

AT THE WORLD TRADE CENTER

As Marine 6 pulled into the marina, I turned around and told my men, "Nobody leaves this boat unless I give the order. Everybody stand fast until you hear from me." I took my aide firefighter, Billy Morrissey, with me and explained that I had to get to the command post and report to let them know that we had the fireboats available. (Billy would survive the attacks of that morning). We jumped off wearing our protective bunker gear and our radios for communication and found the command post about three blocks off Vesey Street on West Street. I reported to the Chief of the Department Pete Ganci, to Ray Downey, Chief in Charge of SOC (Special Operations Command), both close friends of mine, and to 1st Assistant Fire Commissioner Bill Feehan.

I saw Ray and our eyes locked. We knew we were up against a disaster no one had ever experienced before. After years of having worked with him - at Rescue 2, at hurricane disasters in the Caribbean Islands, and in Oklahoma City after the bombing - I knew how he thought. I told him I was anxious to help inside the towers with the evacuation.

"Stay here with me; give me a hand," he said.

"You got it, Boss."

After the second plane attack, a second fifth alarm was transmitted for the South Tower. The land unit companies were reporting in and getting their orders. As the chief in charge of the Marine Division, I had to wait to the side for orders about putting the fireboats into service. The area was becoming crowded with several companies of firefighters reporting in. A decision was made to set up a staging area separate from where the Command Post was located.

The officers waiting for their orders were asked to move to Two Financial Center on West Street at the American Express Building. There was an entrance to an underground parking lot there that had more room. Ray said, "Al, make sure, after the guys get their orders and they know where they're going that you tell them to be careful with secondary devices." The secondary devices he spoke of were other possible explosives, bombs, for instance. Before some of the company officers left, I told them to be extra careful and keep their companies together, and I had a chance to do as Ray had asked and warned them to watch out for any secondary devices.

The situation, as I understood it, was this: we knew we were not going to put this fire out. It was out of control in open areas on several floors. We had a fifth alarm in for the North Tower and a fifth alarm for the South Tower. Because of the massive destruction to the building's infrastructure during the impact, we didn't even know if water could be pumped up to the fire. The primary objective was still to try to evacuate as many civilians as possible and to get as close to the impact area to see if there were any survivors there that we could get out. Operations assumed that there would be a partial and gradual collapse of the floors above the impact and fire area. Although a partial collapse at that height would be devastating in itself, I assumed as I'd imagined the building's designers had, that the lower structure would endure. A worse case scenario was that the top section of the building would topple and we would lose those floors. I knew that we had to do something to help those poor civilians, but we had other major problems to consider as well, rescuing those trapped in the elevators and assisting people in distress, and this included the handicapped. In hindsight, I strongly believe that the Command Post expected that we could evacuate most of the people before any partial collapse would occur.

In the Fire Department, our commitment to life is one of our most basic tenets. I concluded that the Command Post had three major concerns: evacuation of thousands of people from two 110 story high-rises, many needing assistance; rescue of possibly hundreds of those trapped, and finally, preventing the large volume of fires on several floors from impeding the evacuation and rescue efforts. We weren't only fighting the "Red Devil," but the building's construction and damage, and this could hamper our efforts in major ways. This was fast becoming hell.

I remember saying to Ray, "Give me a company or two and get me up there to help put this thing out. We can help get some of these people." I needed to assist in such a desperate time.

"No, Al, we need you here," he repeated. He knew he had to keep me available to command the fireboats because he knew there might be other attacks that could cripple the harbor.

All of a sudden, as I was standing near Ray, I heard a piercing explosion. It sounded like a small bomb. What the hell was that, I wondered. I looked around and saw nothing, so I turned back to the men. And then I heard another dull boom. And another. I looked around again, just as a body fell onto the concrete. Boom! People were jumping to their deaths.

Boom! The bodies hit and exploded. Boom! Boom! I was two blocks away from the Towers, but the sounds made my heart sink. The bodies crashed onto canopies, cars, and the street. The noise was unbearable. Both the sight and sound were sickening and bone-chilling. I've been at fires where people have jumped out of windows to try to save themselves, but this jumping was different. These were the poor innocent souls trapped on those floors above the fires who knew they had to make that horrific choice about death today – to die by fire or by jumping. Boom! Boom! The sounds didn't let up. This was a nightmare that I was to relive in the future.

"Give me a company. Let me get up there," I asked Ray again.

"No. You've got to stay here." He was insistent.

Boom! Boom! People were jumping from all sides of the buildings now. I'm sure they said their prayers and asked God to forgive them for choosing to jump rather than burn to death. I was grateful that those below the fires were starting to evacuate.

As I waited for further orders, I kept looking up every few seconds to see when the next jumpers were coming. I was becoming obsessed with them. Firefighters responding into the Towers had to ensure that a falling body wouldn't strike them. A firefighter or evacuating civilian could be crushed to death. I saw some people jump in groups of three and four, comforting each other for whatever it meant to die by holding hands. I could tell when women jumped by the color of their dresses or when their dresses blew back over their heads in the air. The people were just floating, and then would come that sudden, mind piercing exploding impact. It seemed to take about eight seconds for a person to fall. That was what I saw from my position. Earlier, when I was responding on the fireboat, we had seen some figures jumping, but at that time, the reality hadn't registered. Once I heard the deafening booms of the bodies exploding, it registered.

Firefighters are clearly focused in an emergency. We get past thinking about dangers. We believe in the commitment to life. I can say now that as I stood by the Command Post, I observed that not a single firefighter or officer hesitated about going into the Towers. They received their assignments; some of the officers hand-saluted the chiefs and then they continued on in. They were firefighters; I consider them our first patriots in the war on terrorism.

Jerry Reilly, my good childhood friend from Woodside who also had been in my wedding party, reported in. He was now a lieutenant from 22 Truck in Harlem. He'd received the order to report to the South Tower for further instructions. "Jerry, keep your men together," I told him, as I'd told the officers earlier. "If you can, get the people out, but when it's over, get out." I put my hand on his shoulder to encourage him.

I looked over at another building with a glass lobby and saw that there were some firefighters there, so I went over to check on them. One was Kevin Dowdell from Rescue 4, the Rescue unit stationed in Woodside, Queens. Kevin had been one of my men when I was a lieutenant in Rescue 2. I asked him if everything was okay. "Everything's fine, Al. I just want to have a talk with each of my men." "You've got it, Kevin," I said.

Kevin was always a thorough officer; he fully understood the complexity of the situation, and he wanted his men to be sure of what they were to do.

Other firefighters continued to come in and get their orders; meanwhile, I divided my time between maintaining contact with my fireboats and watching the South Tower, to keep sizing up the situation. Suddenly, I saw on the corner of the building, a bright blue pastel light, very sharp. There was a pop of light and another bright blue light on the other corner, and then another pop of light. Automatically, I thought, secondary devices.

And then, I thought, it's coming down.

"It's collapsing! Run! It's collapsing! It's coming down!" others started screaming.

We knew we weren't directly underneath the tower, but we were close enough that from that height, a section could hit us. There was a clamorous rampage as we ran bumping, pushing and shoving each other towards the underneath driveway. My helmet fell off in the squeeze. I was thinking we didn't have much time.

I ran about ten feet into the driveway, when I came to a dividing wall. In an instant, I turned to my left and crouched down and put my hands over my head. I'm going to die here, I thought, and I started saying the Hail Mary. "Hail Mary, full of grace ..."

There was a sound like a freight train coming – vaaaabooom! As the noise intensified, I intensified my Hail Mary. We were enveloped in this deafening, frightening sound that drowned out my prayer. Everything turned dark on what had been a beautiful bright day. I couldn't breathe. My mouth was full of dust, and it tasted terrible. The noise stopped, and I wondered for a moment if I had died.

My God, the building held! God, I'm alive, I murmured to myself excitedly. I assumed only a part of the building had collapsed. The cloud of dust blocked my vision of all but a couple of inches in front of me. In order to breathe, I drew my mouth inside the collar of my bunker coat to search for some fresh air trapped inside my jacket. I was able to take about two breaths of air, and then started picking myself up.

"All right. All right. Is everybody all right?" a voice asked in the darkness.

"We can get out this way," another voice said. "I think it's a door that leads to a staircase."

We started heading for the door as we could no longer see the driveway entrance, which I was sure was partially blocked by debris anyway. I had no idea of time, but five minutes must have gone by as we searched for our way out. I kept following the beams of flashlights ahead of me. The dust was not the typical black smoke we usually experience at fires, but a choking mixture of particles, soot, ground glass and several other unidentifiable elements. We implemented the lessons we'd learned during our basic fire training classes years before and crouched low, trying to find cleaner air. Finally, someone opened a door and we made our way up the steps. The air was slightly cleaner and we gasped it. When I joined the others outside, I couldn't believe what I saw: crushed cars, debris in ten and twenty foot mounds and that gray chalky dust everywhere.

I bumped into Commissioner Bill Feehan who had been at the Main Command Post. We knew each other from my Rescue 1 days in Manhattan, years earlier.

"Al! Al! Are you all right?" he asked me.

"Yes, Commissioner. We have a lot of people dead here. We've got to start searching," I said, anxiously.

"Take it easy, Al. Take it easy," he said.

His words didn't register, but his concern did. As firefighters well know, there comes a time when we go into a rescue mode of thinking; I was in it now. A firefighter in that mode is on the verge of almost completely disregarding his life. I've got to try to save some people; I've got to try to help, I kept thinking. "I need some men. Give me some men, so we can start searching," I said.

"Yes. All right," he replied.

Two firefighters whom I didn't know came over and said,

"Cap, we're here with you."

"All right. Let's get some tools."

We began rummaging around some half-damaged apparatus, gathering a light and a few tools we could possibly use. We were on Vesey Street, so I started walking back to get to the South Tower. As I made a right, I saw Pete Ganci. Years back, Pete and I had owned a small business together. He'd been assigned as a Battalion Chief in Battalion 57, and I was a Lieutenant in Engine 235, sharing the same quarters in Bedford-Stuyvesant, Brooklyn. Pete just looked at me with a concern that reflected his anguish and the enormity of what had just occurred. We started walking next to each other quietly and turned onto West Street, south, towards the collapse. There were civilians, firefighters and police officers passing us, going north and west towards the Hudson River and the water's edge, seeking refuge, which was naturally the smart thing to do. It was time to leave the area.

We saw that the North Tower, which was the first tower to get hit, was still standing and burning. Most of the people above the fire were dead by now. There was no one jumping. As our small group continued walking, Chief Ray Downey appeared and came alongside me. "Al," he said in a low voice, "we just lost a lot of good men."

"I know, Ray," I told him. "We're going to start searching."

As we continued, Ray said, "Where the #***# are those fighter pilots?"

He was worried about a third plane's coming in for an attack. As the one in charge of strategic operations, he was always one step ahead of many people at an emergency. Earlier when we were at the Command Post, I wasn't aware of it, but he had already called for military air support. Since the military and its airbases had downsized, armed fighter pilots who would normally come from Long Island or New

Jersey, had to fly down from Cape Cod. They arrived in New York City, but eight minutes too late to shoot down the second plane, not that that decision could even have been made, that morning. If it had, and if those pilots had been able to shoot down the second plane, they might possibly have saved hundreds or thousands of lives.

As we continued walking, another chief came over to Ray. I didn't find out until later on that it was Mike Telesca. He had been trapped, but luckily was able to get out from what was left of the ruins of the Marriott Hotel, after the collapse of the South Tower. I believe he mentioned to Ray that there were civilians and firefighters still trapped inside the partially collapsed Marriott.

We could see that the whole 110 stories of the South Tower had fallen completely, in pancake fashion. The scene was one of total devastation, with fires burning everywhere. The place had become a war zone.

This was one of those situations in which there was no going back. From what I remember, it was just Ganci, Feehan, Downey, a couple of firefighters and I walking towards Tower One and what was left of the Marriott Hotel. A few people scurried past us to get away from the gray dust that covered everyone and everything in sight.

As debris kept raining down from the North Tower, which was still standing, I came across a helmet, which a firefighter had lost, and I put it on. It fit too snugly on my head, but it was better than nothing. We made our way over multiples of ten, fifteen and twenty foot mounds of debris on West Street, all of which made our walk slow and very dangerous. We could see approximately six to eight firefighters and civilians who were lined up in what looked like the remains of the Marriott lobby. Often, during routine fire operations, firefighters have to throw smoldering furniture and articles out a window to the street below. As a safety precaution, we station a firefighter outside who directs the firefighters, telling them when to move in or out of the building so that they can avoid being hit by anything.

"Al, I'm going to give them a hand. Stay outside and let me know when I can send them safely out. A lot of debris is still coming down from the North Tower," Ray said.

That was the last time I talked to Ray. I was left standing outside and looking up at the North Tower. I could see a large dark section of structural debris falling, so I raised my hand to stop anybody from moving out; then there was a clearing. Some debris was falling, but not that much. I waved my hand in a frenzy towards myself, signaling Ray that it was okay to come out, but coming out wasn't easy because they had to crawl over a large slab of cement and other debris from the South Tower collapse.

One firefighter did crawl out. It was Brian O'Flaherty, my friend and my old Captain from Rescue 1. He got out in time and proceeded past me. There was no time to even stop to acknowledge him, and I don't think he recognized me, because I had that other firefighter's helmet on. It turned out that Brian was seriously injured from the collapse of the South Tower. One of his shoulders was severely torn and needed medical attention immediately. He moved behind me before any more debris came down.

When it became clear again, I waved again and yelled, "Come on, let's go! Come on! It's clear!" I kept shouting and waving for them to come out, but nobody was moving. What was wrong with them, I wondered. I'd assumed they were hesitating because they were having a problem navigating across that concrete slab, but they seemed preoccupied, so I decided to get closer to see what they were doing. Maybe something else was wrong; maybe they needed a hand. I remember seeing the silhouette of another good friend and working partner, Chief Larry Stack of the Safety Battalion, on the extreme right, so from the middle of West Street, I started heading towards the partially collapsed Marriott to assist. Without any warning, there was the same horrific loud vvaaaaroooooooom! There was no time to run, just to get ready for the impact. In a matter of six to eight seconds, the North Tower collapsed. Everything was over. I was knocked unconscious.

The firefighters and civilians I had been assisting and attempting to evacuate were never found. Some of them were identified through DNA later on; my friend Ray Downey was among them. I don't know how or why I was still alive. I have constantly thought about those seconds and how I was only feet away from being crushed to death.

I have a vague memory of turning, looking up and bracing my left arm over my head to shield myself against a large dark object that was falling fast directly on top of me. My left side suffered the most damage. My skull was severely fractured, several ribs were broken, one puncturing my left lung; my left hand was broken, as were several fingers, and I suffered damage to several vertebrae and discs. I sucked in a lot of dirt and debris in the heavy gray dust cloud that slowly settled over me, and I became hidden under concrete and steel. I became part of the devastation and blended in with the quiet eerie landscape.

This time I was all alone. Everyone around me was dead. There was nobody around to know I was there, partly buried under the debris. All I had was my super radio on my right side. I couldn't move my left arm, as it was partially pinned under some metal and severely injured. When I regained some consciousness, my right arm was free, so I managed to press the transmitting button on the speaker that activates the mike, which was resting near my face. I tried right away, to reach the dispatcher. I don't remember talking on the radio, but my desperate transmissions were recorded.

As my left lung collapsed, my right one filled up with the gray and white chalky dust. Unbeknownst to me, the bottom part of my lungs suffered chemical burns from the mixture of the chemical make-up of the dust and unknown debris. Between the skull fracture and the lack of oxygen in my one lung, I began drifting in and out of consciousness. I was now fighting for my life.

CHAPTER THREE

CHILDHOOD IN AMERICA

It's been said that your life flashes before your eyes when you're about to die. I had time to have several flashes of my life pass before my eyes because I was dying the slow death of asphyxiation, caused by my collapsed lung and by all the dust that had coagulated in the other lung. I did not die in a few seconds the way all the innocent civilians, rescue workers and my 343 brothers had. I was dying between whatever tiny gasps of air my lungs could take in. The worst part of dying this way was not being able to say goodbye – to my wife and children, and other loved ones.

Without enough oxygen, I continued to drift in and out of consciousness. Whenever I came to and squeezed the button on my super radio in an attempt to reach the dispatcher, I hoped he'd be able to make sense of my disoriented thinking, and send help.

Captain Fuentes: ...urgent...

Dispatcher: Unit with an urgent, go ahead ...

Capt. F:	I'm trapped here in the collapse … We have numerous people trapped here from the … collapse …K … we need a hand
D:	Where are you?
Capt. F:	I really don't know …
D:	Where were you operating?
Capt. F:	The West Side …K…
D:	The West Side of Tower Number One or Tower Two?
Capt. F:	Tower one …
D:	All right. Ten-four. Calling the mobile command vehicle… Calling the mobile command vehicle …
Mobile Command:	Mobile Command
D:	I have an urgent message for the staff chief. We have contact with units that are trapped in the vicinity of the West Side of Tower Number One. They are requesting urgent help.

* * * *

The plane was the biggest thing I had ever seen as an eight year old. My father Alfredo, whom we affectionately called

"Popi," had given me the window seat after I had pleaded with him to let me look out. When the engines spat to a start and began their loud roar, I turned to my father and pointed to the spinning propellers. It was impossible to sit still while peering out the window at the disappearing airport, as we climbed above the clouds.

It was January, 1960, and my father, older brother Ricardo, baby sister Adrian, and I were finally leaving Ecuador to join my mother Aida and my younger sister, Elizabeth, in America. Ten months earlier, determined to make a better life than the one we knew, my parents had made the difficult decision to separate the family and have my mother and sister go on ahead. My mother, whom we called "Mima," joined her sister, my Aunt Norma, in New York City. Norma had helped by sending us money from whatever she could save from her factory job in Manhattan, but there was only enough for two to make the trip. After they left, I had begun to dream about going to America too.

Now, we were on our way. At one point during the flight, I got out of my seat to pick up a small toy that had fallen. When I bent down to reach for it, the plane hit an air pocket and dropped. I tried to straighten up, but I felt this enormous weight on my back. That was the first time I'd ever experienced the pressure of gravity. When I finally could straighten up, I was so afraid that I decided to spend the remainder of the flight secure in my seat.

The plane landed in New York City at Idlewilde Airport, which is now Kennedy International Airport. In those days, there were no telescoping ramps that led to the terminal. We came down a staircase right onto the tarmac, adjacent to the terminal. I was gripping one of my father's hands, while two year old Adrian was gripping his other.

Since we didn't own any winter coats, we stepped out and

into our first experience of cold winter air. The climate of Ecuador is mild almost all year round. I'd had no idea that air could get this cold, and I worried about whether or not it was safe to breathe such cold air. As I exhaled, I couldn't believe my eyes. 'Smoke' came out of my mouth.

"Do you see the smoke? Do you see the smoke?" I kept saying, looking at my father and then my older brother to see if they saw what I was seeing. But they were making smoke too. They explained what was happening and told me to calm down. I kept myself busy by experimenting with inhaling the cold air and then exhaling my smoke. After a little while, when I got tired of that, I realized something white was covering the ground. Instinctively, I reached down to touch it, and it felt so cold, I thought that maybe I had burned my hand. Smiling at my bewilderment, my father and Rick tried to explain that this was snow. Cold winter air, smoke and now snow – I had flown into a whole new world. As we walked to the terminal, I continued blowing out onto the air, trying to understand this new phenomenon my own breath could form.

Inside the terminal, my father became more serious and seemed tense. Without understanding English himself, he was trying to get us through Immigration. All I could tell was that someone in a uniform was speaking a funny language, and as my father became more and more nervous, he kept shoving the passports and visas over to the officer. We were at the mercy of the first American any of us had ever met, as I was pretty sure my father had never met an American in Ecuador.

My father had every reason to be tense. We had come so far, had used all of our savings to fly here, and were hoping to see my mother, after such a long separation. Even I understood the importance of this moment, and I was scared too. All I wanted was to hug her and to feel her hugging me. I'd missed her very much and knew she was waiting anxiously for us. The officer finally stamped our passports and signaled us to come through, with a slow wave of his arm.

I was too young to truly understand the significance of that simple gesture, to come on through. I realize now that my parents had made great sacrifices to get us to America. We were literally crossing the threshold from one world into another, leaving one life to enter into a new life. Those born in this country may never know what it means to cry and give thanks to be able to come to America. Even now, whenever I fly into the States, I give thanks that I'm back home.

My mother had no extra money to meet us at the airport, so my father hailed a cab and the four of us piled in and began to explore this place called America. The ride would take us past the tallest buildings I'd ever seen. So many of them, and all squeezed so close together. We crossed a bridge, and there was the breathtaking view of the colossal Manhattan skyline. It looked like a city from Space. As the cab drove us along the Manhattan streets, I wondered how these people could see the sky. I could see only wall-to-wall buildings and had to tilt my head uncomfortably way back to see a little bit of it.

We finally reached our destination – 310 West 99th Street, in Harlem – our new home. Aunt Norma, one of my mother's four sisters, had moved to America eight years earlier, and some time later, had moved into a modest one-bedroom apartment in this large apartment house. During the late 1950's and early 1960's, this upper Manhattan neighborhood consisted of lower middle class people made up of "minorities." Social welfare was common here, but this building had been one of the few places affordable to my aunt, and now, my family. Across the street, there was an apartment building converted into an SRO (Single Room Occupancy), which meant that each person had his own room, but everyone shared a common bathroom. The tenants there were primarily the elderly and the poor, which made for a depressing environment.

This didn't dampen our spirits. We were finally here, and the moment of our arrival and our long anticipated reunion was intense, with my mother crying and hugging all of us. Our baby sister Adrian was only two, and my mother hadn't seen her for the last nine months. We were all together now, finally, and that was what mattered. We couldn't have been a happier family: husband, wife, two daughters and two sons. The only problem, and it was an immediate one, was where to fit all six of us in this one bedroom apartment. (My aunt had moved out to Sunnyside, Queens). It was decided that my father, mother and my two sisters would share the bedroom, while I shared the Castro sofa bed with my brother in the living room.

I was a new immigrant in America; my mother and father had set my dreams in motion. I knew that night, that some of my dreams and bedtime prayers were coming true.

CHAPTER FOUR

NEW YORK CITY, 1960 -
PARENTS' STRUGGLE

Capt. F: ...Urgent ...

D: All right. Stand by. Stand by.
                Unit with urgent, go ...

Capt. F: ... Yeah... This is Marine six ... I'm on the
                West Side Highway ... I'm pinned ...

D: Are you an officer or a firefighter from
                Marine six?

Capt. F: I'm an officer from the Marine Division, K ...

D: You're on the West Side Highway or the west
                side of the building?
Capt. F: ... The highway ...

D: You're on the West Side Highway?

Capt. F: ... I was ... ten-four.

D: All right. We're going to get some members
                            over there to assist you. Calling the mobile
                            command vehicle ...

*   *   *   *

I was extremely happy in the new apartment. What eight-year-old boy wouldn't be happy to have a television for the first time? We'd never owned one in Ecuador, and the only working TV I had ever seen was one at a fair, in my hometown of Guayaquil. It didn't matter that our TV set looked like a large wooden dresser with a small 5 x 7 inch screen in the center. That TV alone made it worth coming to America.

Once we were settled in, the first issue we had to resolve was getting ourselves some winter clothes for the January weather. Money was extremely tight, so someone had told Mother she should go to the Salvation Army Thrift Shop. After finding it, we were soon outfitted in used but warm clothes that helped us brave the cold air sweeping down from Canada through New York City.

Since we'd emigrated in January, my attending school was temporarily put on hold. I began my introduction to English by watching "The Million Dollar Movie" with all its re-runs on our small TV screen. Whenever my mother let me out, I'd run to one particular hill on Riverside Drive, next to the West Side Highway. As a young boy fresh from South America who knew nothing about snow, I learned quickly all the fun I could have bumping and sliding down a snowy hill.

During the day, my mother and her sister Norma worked together at Garays on 14th Street in Manhattan, where they manufactured ladies' quality handbags. Although Garays was called a factory, in actuality, it was one of those notorious sweatshops where women toiled all day, working with heavy leather on commercial sewing machines while being paid "by the piece," meaning so many cents for every handbag sewn. My mother's daily production provided a modest income that paid the rent and got us groceries. The factory had fifty or more women sitting in rows, each working her machine non-stop, sewing leather and suede. A male supervisor would walk around the women at their tables, making sure there was no talking, only production. If a worker needed water, or more material to sew, it was the supervisor's job to get it and bring it to her. A woman was not to interrupt her work, except to take one short break in the morning and another in the afternoon, and a break for lunch.

Aunt Norma had helped my mother get the job. Norma had told the supervisor about a woman she knew – a 'friend' – who needed work. Since the factory rule prohibited the hiring of relatives (probably for fear they would be tempted to talk too much), my aunt didn't share this information. After the supervisor assured Aunt Norma that he would hire her friend if she could work the sewing machine, my aunt told my mother to come to the factory.

"Do you know how to operate one of these machines?" the supervisor asked her in Spanish. That was all that mattered.

"Si," my mother said. She knew how to use a sewing machine, but she had never worked a heavy-duty commercial one like this, and never all day, sewing heavy leather and suede.

After watching her work the machine, the supervisor agreed to hire her. My mother probably couldn't have gotten another job without a rudimentary knowledge of English, so when she got that job at the factory, it was as if God had intended all along, for all of us to come to America. Though tedious and low paying, it offered my mother two things: Aunt Norma's daily companionship as Mother learned about America, and more importantly, enough money over the course of those first nine months, to make a deposit on the airplane tickets for the rest of us to come and join her. That factory job in America made all the difference, because my father was making very little money in Ecuador, at that time.

Still, my mother's first day on the job almost turned into a disaster. Some time during that very first day, she mistakenly moved her hand the wrong way, and the machine's large needle, meant for the leather bag, pierced her palm and protruded out the other side, pinning her hand against the table. Instantly, she held her breath, too afraid to scream for fear of losing the job. My Aunt Norma saw her sister's dilemma, but because she was also afraid to make a scene, kept quiet. Gloria, a Puerto Rican woman who sat next to my mother (the same woman who had suggested the thrift shop) saw what had happened and immediately came to her aid. She began working the needle slowly in reverse, until it pulled back out of my mother's hand. Once the needle was out, my mother went on working as if nothing had happened. She was perspiring heavily from both fear and pain, but the thought of being discovered kept her going. It wasn't until her one-hour lunch break that my mother finally attended to the hand. She wrapped it and then went back to work for the rest of the day. This is one of our family stories, but it shows my mother's fortitude and determination to let nothing stop her from bringing her family to America. Gloria became and remains a life-long friend.

Although we were all here now, we began to realize that the transition was not going to be easy. My father didn't know English. He did go out looking for work every day, but then he would return, having found nothing, at least, not in his field of accounting or bookkeeping. The only jobs open to someone like him, with his lack of English were those of short order cook or dishwasher, both of which he considered too demeaning.

After months of his unemployment, my mother became uneasy. She suggested that if he couldn't find work, we should move back to Ecuador. Life here was becoming more and more expensive, and working in the factory too difficult, while trying to provide for six people.

When I heard this, I thought, go back where? Guayaquil? But what would we go back to?

In spite of the fact that Guayaquil in the 1950's was the country's largest city, making a living there was difficult. Life was difficult all over Ecuador at that time. The country's main exports were rice and chocolate, both commodities vulnerable to weather extremes of too much heat or rain. The petroleum and banana industries were underdeveloped; companies were going bankrupt, and thousands of people were unemployed. Ecuador's economy was suffering from the gross proportions of inflation.

My father had started his accounting-bookkeeping career in Ecuador working for an accounting firm that provided services for several banks in the city, but as the economy worsened, many of these banks failed. Since he was the youngest, and a newcomer, my father was one of the first to be let go. With Ricky's and my additional mouths to feed, my father looked for new work, so that he could provide for his growing family, but he could get only temporary modest jobs, like maintaining the accounting books for a local store. And nothing paid well.

As happens with many good practicing Catholics, my parents then had another baby. The family continued to grow, but we were a financially stressed family in a financially stressed country. In time, my father found a job three hours outside Guayaquil at a hacienda, where he maintained the books and did the accounting for the farm business. The job offered the benefits of a private house and food, but again, little pay. A year later, I was ready to start school, but since there were no decent schools in this rural setting, my parents moved us back to Guayaquil to live at Aunt Edga's house. Here, I was enrolled at San Jose, a Catholic grammar school run by the Silesian order, where I would receive a proper education. We always paid our share of expenses at my aunt and uncle's house, but privacy and a sense of dignity were lacking. This is when I'd begun to hear my parents mention that strange word – 'America.' How could we ever go back to Ecuador, now?

As my father struggled to find work, and we continued to live on a meager budget, I began to realize the sacrifices my parents had made to get us to this little apartment in West Harlem. As a child, I felt a tremendous responsibility not to fail in America, because if I did, how could I ever face them?

On those days when my mother went off to work and Father went looking for work, a neighbor babysat for us, but one day, Mother couldn't find us when she returned home. Terrified, she began searching the building and finally rang the superintendent's doorbell. He opened the door, smiled and waved her in. To her surprise, she found us there, eating. One of us had said something to him about how hungry we were, so the good-natured super, understanding our dilemma, wanted to help. My mother thanked him in Spanish for his kindness, but felt terribly embarrassed that he would think she wasn't feeding us properly. She collected us together and guided her little ones back to our apartment.

Through constant perseverance and help from a friend, my father finally landed a mail clerk's job at a steamship company named Gran Colombiana, the shipping agents for a firm in Colombia, South America. At that company, he could get by speaking his native Spanish and was expected to learn some English as he went along, so he was more than willing to take the job. Eventually, he was promoted to account clerk and was transferred to Pier #3 in the Red Hook section of Brooklyn, where the vessels dry-docked and unloaded their products. He continued working for this firm for thirty years, until he was forced to retire. During his retirement, he was re-hired to work for the company at their new offices in The World Trade Center, a part-time job he kept for three years.

It was while living on 99th Street that I witnessed my first fire and New York City's firefighters, (bomberos in Spanish) in action. There was always something happening in the SRO dwelling across the street, and on this particular day, smoke was billowing out one of its windows. As I heard the sirens grow louder and louder, I ran outside to see red fire trucks with bright red lights flashing, making their way up the street. When they stopped in front of the SRO and the fire, I was amazed at all the activity. An aerial ladder was raised imme-diately, and sent directly to the apartment window, and fire-fighters started climbing it. They seemed fearless as they entered a window and disappeared into the dark smoke. Those trapped inside were found and brought to the window and helped down the ladder. The other bomberos were carry-ing fire hoses through the front door. It looked like 'organized chaos,' and I was so impressed because people had been res-cued and the building was safe.

My mother never liked the SRO hotel across the street. She never really cared for the neighborhood. As my older brother Rick started making new friends, she grew increas-ingly concerned. She was afraid that these new kids were too tough. The boys hung out in large groups, and looked like the gangs that were always on the TV news. As a concerned mother, she felt Rick's association with tough kids meant that only trouble lay ahead. The reality was that he had also found a job at the same factory where she and my aunt worked. At the tender age of sixteen, my brother Rick was working full time. He was a provider, assisting with alleviating the financial burdens on the family. Eventually, he received his high school degree and served in the United States Armed Forces, in the armored tank division. I owe my brother a great deal.

If we had ever doubted it before, we didn't any longer, the neighborhood was changing. One night, we heard a commotion; then the sound of gunshots rang out across the street in the SRO. My parents were disturbed that gunshots were becoming more and more frequent. "We didn't come here to live like this," they both said, and the decision was made to search for a better neighborhood.

CHAPTER FIVE

WOODSIDE, QUEENS

Marine 6:	Marine six to Manhattan.
D:	Marine six.
Marine 6:	The member you just spoke to is Captain Fuentes. He is the Marine Division.
D:	I'm trying to get him some help. Calling the mobile command vehicle...
Engine 28:	Engine twenty-eight. Ten-four.
D:	Twenty eight Engine.
Engine 28:	Where do you have members trapped? K...
D:	Where are you twenty-eight engine?
Engine 28:	Where?
D:	They're on the West Side Highway opposite the

	World Trade Center. We have Captain Fuentes trapped …
Engine 28:	Ten-four.
Marine 6 alpha:	Marine six alpha to Manhattan. K…
D:	Marine six alpha.
Marine 6 alpha:	Where do you want us?
D:	Marine six alpha. Where are you right now?
Marine 6 alpha:	We're inbound the Brooklyn Navy Yard.
D:	Start out for lower Manhattan opposite the World Trade Center.

*   *   *   *

Aunt Norma was living in a small apartment in Sunnyside, a neighborhood across the East River, in the borough of Queens, when my parents and she decided to look for another place and move in together. This way they could share the expenses on a better apartment in a better neighborhood. We ended up renting the first floor of a two-family house, in Woodside, Queens. At the time, Woodside was a predominantly Irish neighborhood, with a few other nationalities mixed in. Hispanics, in the 1960's, were really a minority. What a difference from the days I'd known back at my uncle's house in Ecuador.

I fondly remember when my aunts, uncles and cousins would get together for a barbecue fiesta at my uncle's hacienda in the mountains. I used to play with the horses and farm animals, as well as watch what I deemed the cruel practice of cutting off a chicken's head and plucking off the feathers, in preparation for dinner. I loved eating the food cooked outside on the pit, but I stopped watching the animals get slaughtered.

The hacienda had a river that ran through the land, and as children, we would go swimming there, or watch the green iguanas jump from the high tree branches into the water. Whenever an iguana would jump near us, we'd run out of the water screaming, afraid that it wanted to bite us. The truth was that it only wanted a fish. Those days on the pristine land of the hacienda and those nights of looking at the stars had turned into memories.

My life now consisted of row houses, concrete everywhere except in a few parks, and the eardrum-piercing screeching brakes and scraping metal wheels of the Number 7 elevated train that rumbled overhead along Roosevelt Avenue through Woodside. I could consider myself a New York street-smart kid now; I lived a world away from the world I had known in Ecuador.

I remember my mother's telling me each week, "You have to help your father go shopping for meat and groceries." We couldn't afford to go to the regular A& P, as prices were too high, so we would take the Number 7 to Time Square and then change for the uptown train to "La Marqueta" on 125th Street in Harlem, where there was an open meat market under the trestle. We would buy just enough meat to last us a week or two. On the way home, the bags were so heavy that we had to stop and rest every two blocks. I could only wonder how my relatives were enjoying their weekends at the hacienda, as I trudged back with my bags filled with meat and chicken.

That September, after we moved to Woodside, I entered the third grade at P.S. 11. Although I had learned some English words in my grammar school in Ecuador, I really couldn't speak the language at all, so I forced myself to learn it as quickly as possible because I knew this would be vital in order to make friends and fit in. One of my first real friends in Woodside was Tom Costello. I had become sick in school one day, and Tom volunteered to walk me home. We weren't close; he just saw it as an opportunity to get out of class. Still, we became good friends, and years later, he would be in my wedding party, and I in his.

Besides making friends and acquiring a formal education, I had my first lessons in prejudice at P.S. 11. On Thursdays, the students and teachers would gather for assemblies. One student would be chosen to carry the American flag down the aisle and up the steps to the stage; then everyone would perform the Pledge of Allegiance. I was so impressed by this that I asked one of the teachers in my broken English, if I could carry the flag. More than anything, I wanted to carry that flag.

"Absolutely," she said. I remember picking it up and feeling so proud, but no sooner had I started up the aisle than another teacher stepped out and stopped me. "What is he doing carrying the flag?" she said, looking around.

This was my first experience with prejudice. I couldn't understand all the words, but I understood the feeling. The teacher grabbed the pole from me. I've never forgotten that moment or the hurt. The other teacher came to my aid, when she saw me crying, and to this day, I wish I knew her name. She stood up for me and argued with the other teacher on my behalf. "How can you do this?" she asked her. Nevertheless, I didn't get to carry the flag that day or any other day, and I no longer wanted to. I felt embarrassed, humiliated in front of everyone, and far from accepted. But it didn't stop me from wanting to be in America.

Some boys I'd met and liked attended another school in Woodside, so with the memory of that nice Catholic school in Ecuador, I took a walk down to this other school – St. Sebastian's – and knocked on the principal's door.

"Can I help you?" a nun asked, looking down at me.

I had learned just enough English to tell her that I wanted to attend St. Sebastian's.

She smiled and asked, "Where are your parents?"

I explained that they were working, and then told her again that I really would like to attend school there, and that I wanted my sisters to be able to also.

The nun took a liking to me and took down my phone number and address. A few days later, someone came by the house and asked my parents if they knew that I'd been at the school and that I wanted to enroll there.

"Yes, we know, but we can't afford it," my parents said in their broken English.   Somehow, partial payments were worked out, and the following September, my sisters and I started at St. Sebastian's. It worked out perfectly for me, and I started to flourish there.

Even there, though, prejudice made its presence known. I was the "different one." Again, most of my classmates were of Irish descent, and while I had friends, some of my class-mates considered it their mission to indoctrinate me into the neighborhood. I would be in the schoolyard playing, and some other boy would try to bully me by calling me a "spic." Others would pick up on the word and start calling out in a singsong, "Spic and Span. Spic and Span." One day, when the teasing didn't let up, I decided to confront the boy who'd started the name-calling. We got into a fight and I wound up punching him. Both of us learned a hard lesson that day, but the result was that we became friends; we're still friends. I realized that I had to stand up for myself to gain some respect. I also realized that if prejudice were going to exist, I'd have to take a positive attitude and make it work for me. Every knock is a boost, I'd tell myself, and I actually believed that. Every time someone discriminated against me, I made myself a promise that I'd show that person how much better I was than what he or she thought about me.

But prejudice has its more painful moments too. When I was about fifteen, I met a blond haired girl whom I asked out on a date. When I arrived at her house and knocked on the door, her father answered and took a good look at me.

"Hello, is Susan home?" I asked.

"Wait a minute," he said, and closed the door. I waited, expecting Susan to come out, when all of a sudden, I heard yelling. I stood there for about ten minutes. When the door finally opened, Susan appeared. She'd obviously been crying. "My dad doesn't want me to go out with you," she said.

I turned and went home heartbroken. Once again, I realized that I was 'the other' in this fair-skinned Irish neighborhood, and I learned that I wasn't always going to be accepted. Did the experience hurt me? Absolutely. It killed me. My identity was forming, and I started looking in the mirror to try to figure out what was wrong with me.

One day I approached my mom and said, "Mom, I have to get my hair straighter."

"Don't worry about your hair. You're fine," she told me.

But I didn't believe her, so I decided to experiment with "improving" myself by taking the advice of some friends. I broke open some eggs and mixed the eggs into my hair, to dry overnight. The next morning, I couldn't chisel my hair apart. It took some time, but I slowly began to realize that I had to live with what God had given me.

And for all the times that I met up with prejudice, there were those others when people were good to me; in fact, having grown up in that neighborhood, I came to have more lifelong Irish friends – friends with names like Keilty, Reilly, Clancy, Quinn, Costello and Kiernan – than Hispanic.

One of the greatest influences on me was the Woodside Boys' Brigade, run by Eddie Fowley. Eddie was a sincere and dedicated man who wanted to give the Woodside boys a sense of character, and keep them from hanging around drinking and getting into trouble on the streets.

Every Friday evening, the Brigade met in the basement of St. Sebastian's. We would pledge allegiance and salute the flag and practice marches and drills in this semi-military organization. Twice a year, we traveled to Washington, D.C. where we stayed at the U.S. Marine barracks. It was inspiring to meet others who had this love of country. I began to realize a new sense of pride in America with the Woodside Boys' Brigade.

This isn't to say that Eddie and the other leaders of the Brigade weren't your typical down-to-earth normal people. They occasionally tipped a few too many beers at Shelly's Bar (which Ed Fowley owned), but they were good people and good examples to us. I was never treated differently in the Brigade; I was one of the platoon. Although Eddie Fowley died a few years ago, the Woodside Boys' Brigade still carries on, led in part, by men who had previously been members there years ago. It's produced some outstanding individuals, including an Assistant Director of the FBI.

The Vietnam War made a major impact on all of American society, and Woodside wasn't spared. After the war ended, it was noted that Woodside had produced the most medal winners in Vietnam, including two Congressional Medal winners, a few Silver Star winners and several other meritorious medals awardees. Unfortunately, Woodside also suffered the most deaths of any area in the country, and while many of us believed strongly in our country, a darker side to the Vietnam War began to emerge. As was happening throughout this land of ours, Vietnam veterans were coming home broken in spirit. Walter Berry, or "Bubba" as we called him, was a close friend. He wrote to me many times from Nam, but of all his letters, one particular one stuck in my mind. In it, he said to tell all the kids from the neighborhood not to enlist, not to go to Nam. "It's hell," he wrote. At that time, another friend and I had been considering enlisting, but Bubba's letter and the overall mood of the country made me stop and reconsider.

Bubba had affectionately been dubbed "the mayor" of Woodside. He was fun loving, and just a wonderful person to be around, someone you could always depend on. Everybody knew him, and he'd made it a point to know everybody, always keeping a special watch over the younger kids in "his" town. We had learned to listen to what he said. In time, Bubba came back from Nam, but he wasn't the same. I don't think he ever told anyone everything that he'd experienced there. He lived in mental and physical pain, and eventually all the pain killed him.

Woodside has had its heroes in another war too, the war on fire. In June of 2001, the F.D.N.Y. lost three firefighters on Father's Day in a fire at a hardware store in Astoria, Queens. We called it "The Father's Day Massacre." All three of those men – my friend Harry Ford who lived in my town of Long Beach; Brian Fahey, and John Downing – had ties to Woodside. Each of them worked in Woodside firehouses: L-163 and Rescue Co. 4, and John came from Woodside; I coached him when he was a kid.

This was Woodside, a town made up of hard-working blue-collar families whose children typically became police officers, firefighters or workers in the construction industry.

They all believed in country; they all believed in community; they all believed in New York City. Woodside and the fine people I met while growing up there – some Irish, some from other ethnic backgrounds - are largely responsible for the person I am today.

CHAPTER SIX

F.D.N.Y.

Mobile Command

Vehicle:	Repeat your message. You got cut off, Manhattan.
D:	Broadway and Vesey reported to be the new command post. Broadway and Vesey. Get that information to car three or car five.
MCV:	Be advised I have Chief Nigro in the vehicle at this time.
D:	All right. Ten-four. Advise Chief Nigro.
Capt. F.:	…I'm under the collapse …
D:	Other unit calling Manhattan.
Capt. F.:	unintelligible … we need some help here…
D:	What unit?

Capt. F.:	unintelligible … we need the collapse unit … this is Captain Fuentes. A couple of other members … K …
D:	Are you trapped, Captain? Captain Fuentes, are you trapped?
Capt. F.:	Ten-four.
MCV:	Mobile Command to Manhattan, K.
D:	Go ahead, Mobile Command.

*   *   *   *

With the military no longer a professional option, but with graduation approaching, it was time to start thinking about looking for a 'real' job. When a friend's father informed me that the Plumbers' Union #2 (Manhattan and the Bronx) would be offering the test, I took it. The New York City Local #2 Plumbers' test focused primarily on logical and mechanical reasoning. I scored very well, coming out sixteenth on the list, and while the federal government was urging companies at that time, to hire "minorities," I was told by the company that hired me (Meredith-Heally & Halloran) that I'd have been chosen to work for the firm anyway.

As an apprentice for the plumbing trade, and under union rules, I had to attend plumbing school once a week for five years, after which I would be classified a 'journeyman' or mechanic. I attended school on Monday nights in the South Bronx. All the students took turns standing guard outside; if we didn't, we'd come out from class to find our car batteries, radios and sometimes even out cars stolen.

My employer had me working with the construction of Sloan Kettering Hospital in New York City and the VA Hospital in the Bronx, and my apprenticeship was coming to an end. I was just about to start making an excellent salary, getting full mechanic's pay in the Plumbers' Union, when the New York City Fire Department called to say that I was being drafted to serve, if I were still interested.

After I had taken the F.D.N.Y. entrance test in 1970, the city had gone into a hiring freeze, but now it was time to make a career decision. I'd always wanted to work in a profession that wasn't just demanding in a physical sense, but that also served a decent and honorable purpose. I remembered the heroic actions of those firefighters when I was living on 99th Street, and I felt honored and excited that I would be a probationary firefighter (proby) who some day would be working alongside them. While I may have been a little idealistic and naïve, taking a thirty percent pay cut and turning down the Plumbers' Union, I believed strongly that becoming a New York City firefighter meant working in the greatest fire department in the world.

On September 24th, 1977, I was sworn in as a probationary firefighter in the New York City Fire Department. My mother and my then girlfriend, Eileen, attended the ceremony. I remember how my mother who didn't speak much English and Eileen who didn't speak Spanish smiled at each other for most of the day.

"The Rock," an affectionate name for the F.D.N.Y.'s Training Academy, was located on Randall's Island. At the time, the academy was a relatively new and modern firefighting facility, composed of different buildings. Each building replicated a particular type of construction that we might encounter in the city: private dwelling, tenement, commercial building, all except of course, the high-rise.

During the six weeks, the instructors made it clear that we were only probies and that made us lower than dog squat. We weren't to talk to an instructor unless spoken to, and we were to move out of the way, salute and stand still, should a 1st grade firefighter or instructor pass by. It was a semi-military department, and we trained with this in mind. Many of the instructors had been chosen because of their seniority and past experiences with fires, but a military background and the ability to yell loudly and command respect were considered assets. The instructors were constantly on top of us in order to instill the crucial importance of following orders and maintaining a sense of comradeship. We had to learn to depend on each other as a team. The F.D.N.Y. is a family with a great tradition, and we were expected to meet its standards from the start.

Our course of study was extensive. We were taught the principles of fire behavior, the behavior of fire in different types of construction, principles of fighting fires, teamwork, first-aid, water pressures, arson investigation and hazardous materials, to name just a portion of the program. One important thing we learned was to maintain a personal discipline when under unusual and extremely difficult circumstances. That personal discipline and knowledge of fire behavior would, the Department hoped, keep us alive. It became clear that in spite of all our learning, the real learning would have to come on the job. I looked forward to getting through the six weeks because I knew this was going to be a job I was going to love.

CHAPTER SEVEN

FIREFIGHTING

On November 7th, 1977, I was assigned to Engine 1 (E-1) which shared quarters with Ladder 24 (L-24), located at 31st Street between Sixth and Seventh Avenues in the borough of Manhattan. This sharing of space constitutes what is known as a "double house." Although this wasn't as busy an assignment as I would've liked, it provided a good start.

I encountered my first DOA (Dead On Arrival) while working at E-1. Early on a Saturday morning, we were called to a fire at the Chelsea Hotel on West 23rd Street. The fire was on the second floor, and one apartment was fully involved. When we arrived, the residents of the hotel had already awakened from their deep sleep and were beginning to evacuate. We had moved in with the charged line and had begun pushing the fire from the hallway back into the original apartment, when I stumbled over something. I looked down and realized that it was a body. I'm not sure why the person never made it out; he might've died from smoke inhalation. At the time, I was in the company only about two months, and I was upset that we hadn't been able to save him. I learned a lesson about the importance of response time that day. After putting out the fire, our company officer had us new men "package" the individual into a body bag, and later, as the proby, I had the duty of thoroughly cleaning the body bag of bodily fluids and dirt. When we returned to quarters, we analyzed the fire for what we had done well and for what we could improve upon the next time. Every fire, I learned, had a lesson to teach us.

Engine 1 and Ladder 24 are located directly across the street from St. Francis of Assisi Church and Friary. Father Julian "Jules" Deeken, our much-loved chaplain lived at the friary; his official F.D.N.Y. chaplain's car had its garage inside our house. Over the years, Father Deeken and I became good friends. We did a lot of talking at the firehouse, about the job. He was a "buff," ready to go to a fire regardless of the time or the location. If there was a fire, the good father always showed up to help. I recall one fire during which I was stretching the line inside a building, when it suddenly became lighter and much easier to carry. Looking back to see what was happening, I found Father Deeken helping to "push" the line in. Thinking it best to keep him away from any danger, I kindly thanked him and had him move back.

It was Father Deeken who officiated at Eileen's and my wedding, and eventually christened our three children. He would come out to dinner at our home in Long Beach, and our friendship grew deep over the years. When we heard he was sick with terminal cancer, Eileen wrote to him at his sister's house in Florida, where he'd gone for a final rest. He died there a short time later. During my twenty-six years on the job, I always kept a picture of Father Deeken in my F.D.N.Y. locker for support.

After his death, we had another chaplain, a "proby" from the same friary, Father Mychal Judge. Father Judge was a special chaplain who also befriended all the firefighters, a generous, self-sacrificing man of God.

After spending almost two years at Engine 1, I decided to broaden my experience by transferring across the floor to Ladder 24, the truck company. I then worked there for another three years. While at L-24, I started learning more about the "trade" from the senior men in the companies. I refer to 'men' because women hadn't yet been admitted into the department. At L-24, I met great seasoned firefighters like Ronnie Rotter and Dominic Camastro. I began learning through their experience. This F.D.N.Y. tradition of passing down knowledge to younger firefighters by the senior men was truly an excellent way to learn.

Part of L-24's area included the fur district and other commercial occupancies, several of which had formidable doors. These doors, designed in such a way as to keep them from being broken into by thieves, created a challenge for us firefighters whenever we had to make a forced entry to reach a fire or to attend to an emergency. In time, I learned that many of the L-24 firefighters were experts at opening these doors.

We were taught traditional locksmith techniques which could allow us faster entry and at the same time minimize damage. Many of these firefighters carried a small pouch in their pockets, in which they had tiny, specialized tools normally used only by dentists or locksmiths. I've often thought that had the expert lock-pickers among them not chosen the fire department as their career, they would have made expert thieves.

There are always the fires that stand out in one's mind. One of these occurred on June 14th, 1979, when I was working the day tour. Both E-1 and L-24 responded to the fire, which was at Macy's Department Store on 34th Street, in Manhattan. Working that tour with me were two other firefighters from my proby academy class assigned to the same firehouse: Gary Courtney and Walter "Smitty" Smith, a veteran of the Vietnam War. We were third grade firemen with just two years on the job. The fire was reported to be on the fifth floor. When we got there, we began to gain entry, vent and search for the seat of the fire. We found ourselves in a large retail area in heavy smoke conditions, unaware that super heated gases were accumulating at the ceiling, approximately 18 to 20 feet above us. There were mazes of aisles and showcases in various departments, typical of a Manhattan department store of this size. We went in about fifteen feet – I was assisting in hand stretching a two and a half inch line – and after turning left at an aisle, we proceeded approximately another six feet.

In seconds, we had a flash over fire that covered the entire fifth floor. The super heated smoke at the ceiling level had instantaneously converted into fire. All the mannequins and display cases around us were exploding in the engulfing flames. Everywhere I looked, there was fire; we were surrounded by it. The captain in charge started barking the command, "Back out! Back out!"

At that point, we couldn't see which way was out. I hit the ground and grabbed the hose line. I knew that the hose line would lead to the door, out to the hallway, and into the stairwell. In the chaos, I asked myself, which way do I follow the line to get out?

A wrong choice would have me following the line further into the fire. I was now kissing the floor and hoping that the direction I was moving in was toward the door. I had my hands under the extra hose, and while sliding them along as quickly as possible, I kept hoping I wouldn't drop it. This was not the time to lose my sense of direction. My ears started burning, and I thought I was going to die there.

All of a sudden, I saw a cloudy, lighter haze. I dove for this fraction of light, rolling and stumbling over other firefighters who had just made it out into the stairwell. We took a quick roll call to make sure that everyone had made it out. Confusion and denial can often play a role in critical situations. Some of us thought we were all out, but I believe it was the lieutenant who kept saying there was one man still inside.

The lieutenant was right. One of us didn't make it out. All the while, Smitty had been a little ahead of us. I can only guess that when he saw the fire behind us, he tried exiting the other way. We made a desperate attempt to extinguish the fire and find him, but there were several problems. We had no water pressure, so it took some time before we were able to set up enough large caliber water streams to finally put it out, and the retail area was unusually large and complex, stretching from one city block to another. We learned later, that the day before the fire, plumbers had been working on the sprinkler system and had shut off some valves to the fire area.

When Smitty was found, I didn't want anyone but the firefighters in his company to touch him. Gary, our other classmate at the academy, had already been removed to the hospital with severe burns. We put in a call to the chaplain, and Father Deeken responded. It was so good to see him at this time of despair. When he arrived, I felt an unusual sense of peace and comfort come over me. He blessed Smitty and led us in a prayer. The moment seemed unreal - praying in this burned out floor area, tears filling my eyes - I couldn't believe that a friend of mine, a firefighter, had died fighting this blaze. I was angry and confused and extremely sad. I had no idea at that time how many such situations and tears lay ahead of me.

After our service, a group of firefighters from E-1, L-24 and Rescue 1 delicately and with the utmost respect, carried our brother out to the street to the waiting ambulance. This real and sober moment hit me hard. I cried that night and for days afterward, trying to make sense out of what seemed so senseless. The next day, without interruption, the company was at work again. There was a departmental funeral and burial; I thought about Smitty's wife Lorraine and their young beautiful daughters and how they would miss him. Smitty was a good man, a good firefighter, a good father and a good American who had served his country. He deserved more time among us.

Some friends from the academy resigned after that fire. I more than ever wanted to remain in the profession, but I committed myself to learning how to be a better firefighter.

CHAPTER EIGHT

PROMOTIONS AND COMPANIES

Mobile Command:	What units do you have at Broadway and Vesey, at this time?
D:	Unknown, K. We're not sure. We're going to have to send somebody over there. Also, be advised that we are in radio contact with Captain Fuentes and his people. They are trapped. They are trying to give me a location, but he's unable to.
Mobile Command:	All right. Ten-four. As I say, Chief ... is on his way up with members. He's trying to get to them now. Mobile Command Center, K. We're going to head out to Broadway and Vesey. K.
D:	Ten four. Calling Captain Fuentes ...
Capt. F:	... static ... ah ... Ten-four (in pain) ...

D: Is this Captain Fuentes?

Capt. F: Ten-four.

D: All right. We have help on the way to you, Cap. We believe that you're in the west side of the number one World Trade Center in front of the collapse zone. Is that correct?

Capt. F: Inside the collapse zone. Ten-four.

D: All right. We're sending you some help. Seven Engine: Engine Seven to Ladder One members. We received that message. We're on our way. Let him know.

D: Seven Engine and One Truck members are on their way, and the Staff Chief is aware of your location, Cap. Stand by and we'll be there in a little while

Capt. F: ...static...

*   *   *   *

After having spent a few years assigned to L-24, I became interested in moving on and transferring to Rescue Co. 1, in the borough of Manhattan. A Rescue Company differs in responsibilities from the regular Engine and Ladder companies. More extensive training is required, especially in the use of specialized equipment. In addition to firefighting, the Rescue Company is responsible for the rescue of firefighters as well as civilians, in the most difficult situations. These rescues often involve complicated circumstances, extrication from automobiles and machinery, for example. Scuba operations in the rivers and other waterways surrounding greater New York City are also a part of the Rescue Company's responsibilities, and Rescue Companies respond to working fires in the entire borough.

I had made my intentions clear to the Captain of R-1, Brian O'Flaherty, and he and other members of the company had then begun observing me at many of the emergencies that our companies responded to together. One person who approached Brian and facilitated my being considered was Anthony Mauro, a covering captain in Ladder 24 who spoke on my behalf. Another person who might've helped in getting me considered was Jimmy Rogers. I'd eventually follow Jimmy as a firefighter in Rescue 1 and as a Lieutenant in Rescue 2 in Brooklyn, but until this particular day, we hadn't met.

Rescue 1 and L-24 were operating at a fire on 7th Avenue and 29th Street. I was forcing entry on the second floor to get into the apartment, and while up there, we experienced a large explosion in the store below. Everyone evacuated, but when I realized it was safe, I returned to continue to get entry into the apartment to make sure no one was in there. The hallway was charged with smoke and it was impossible to see.

"Is anybody else here?" I heard a voice ask.

"Yeah," I said.

"Do you have an axe?" he asked.

"Yeah."

"Here. Hit over here." He had a halligan, a tool that we use for prying open doors. Hitting the halligan on the head drives the tool into the doorjamb and then the door can be pried open. We finally popped the door, made a search, found nobody there, and came out.

When we got to the street, the other firefighter asked,

"Who was up there with me?"

   "It was me," I said.

   "What's your name?"

   "Al Fuentes. What's yours?" I asked.

   "Jimmy Rogers."

In time, I was officially transferred to Rescue Co. 1, and I gained such valuable experience there, working at so many and various types of fires and emergencies. The men I worked with there were, and still are, some of my closest friends, men like Brian O'Flaherty, Jack "Spanky" McAllister, Bob Burns, John Driscoll, George Kreusher, Bill Bessman. And the list goes on; there are too many great men to mention here, but failure to include their names does not mean that I think of them as any less important or profound an influence on my life. At R-1, I matured as a firefighter and acquired a love for the job that increased with time.

After nine and a half years on the job, and an exhaustive amount of studying, I passed the test for Lieutenant and was promoted. I had two desires at that time: first, I wanted to continue as an officer with a Rescue Company, and secondly, I wanted to work in Brooklyn. I had grown tired of the traffic congestion that caused problems when answering emergency calls in Manhattan, or the continual Class E's, the electrical false alarms in high-rises that seemed to go off, all the time.

Brooklyn is unusually large. It's been said that if Brooklyn were a city, it would be the fifth largest in the nation. Instead of high-rises, many of the buildings there were three stories, and there was less traffic congestion, so we could get to the fires and people faster. There was also more action there. Since officers are assigned to Battalions, one of my wishes was granted when I received my assignment to Battalion 28, which was in Brooklyn. Brooklyn had two divisions then, the

11th and the 13th. I covered the 11th and occasionally Harlem, in Manhattan, and during this period, I learned about the different neighborhoods and the different companies fighting fires in the other boroughs.

Eventually I was assigned to Engine 235, a single engine company on Monroe Street, in what we called Bed Stuy, the Bedford Stuyvesant section of Brooklyn. For a few years, this was the busiest Engine Company in the city. The firefighters there were self-motivated and full of pride, a wonderful group of people with whom to work.

Engine 235 is memorable for a few reasons: it quartered Battalion 57, and one of the chiefs of the 57 was Pete Ganci who would become not only a good friend, but in the near future, the Chief of the Department highest uniform ranking officer of the New York City Fire Department, E-235 also had Lois Mungay. Women were starting to become firefighters, and this sometimes caused problems in the firehouses, as the men sometimes refused to accept them. Many of the men felt the women had gotten the jobs as a result of a lawsuit, and were being placed in houses not because they belonged, but because a judge had ordered it so. I was concerned that Lois might have problems, but I was wrong. Lois was an excellent firefighter, and the men were great about accepting her, and had no trouble speaking their mind, if some other company didn't see it that way. Lois still works there, in one of the busiest companies in the city, and I'm glad to add her as a "sister" to all the "brothers" who have been such excellent firefighters and friends.

In order to have a well-rounded career, I applied to be an officer of a truck. I was temporarily transferred to Ladder 102 on Bedford Avenue, in Brooklyn, and wasn't there six months, when Hurricane Hugo hit Puerto Rico, in 1989. With winds reaching up to 200 miles an hour, Hugo was a Category Five hurricane that left some parts of the island devastated.

To contend with the aftermath of Hugo, Jimmy Rogers was involved in putting together a team to assist the people of Puerto Rico. By now, he'd been promoted from a lieutenant in Rescue 2 to the Captain of Rescue 1. Jimmy called me up and said, "Al, would you like to go with me to Puerto Rico?"

"I'd love to do that," I said.

Ray Downey, Captain of Rescue 2 at the time, was to come with us. Ray was already a legend in the department.

Jimmy Rogers, Ray Downey and I were flown on a C5A military plane, one of the largest planes in the world. There were also about twenty NYPD officers, and we took along nine vehicles. We constituted the NYC team sent to Puerto Rico to help as best we could.

We eventually wound up on the beautiful and small island of Culebra, which is next to Vieques, the island used by the United States Navy for war games and bombing practice, and were scheduled to be there for a week. Mosquitoes are an almost inevitable consequence of heavy rains and storms on tropical islands. As soon as I stepped onto Culebra after the onslaught of Hurricane Hugo, I found it was infested with mosquitoes, and thousands of them wanted to feed on me. I was fortunate in having the Navy rescue me by providing me with repellent.

I've said many times that in my career, there were only two real captains I worked with in the F.D.N.Y., that is, leaders I totally respected and admired, who acted as my mentors and who were instrumental in shaping the way I behaved and viewed the job. These were Brian O'Flaherty and Ray Downey. The first time I met Ray remains a memorable story.

While in Puerto Rico for the Hugo disaster, I was driving the F.D.N.Y. Battalion car that we'd had flown in with us. Ray was sitting in the front passenger seat and Jimmy was in the back. As we were turning onto a bridge, I backed into and slightly struck a part of the bridge. It was no big deal, and there was no damage.

Ray turned to me and said, "Hey fucko. Watch what you're doing."

Ray, a former Marine, had a reputation for being one tough individual, and I found him to be one of the toughest guys I'd ever met in my life. Here I was, a lieutenant, with these two captains. "What did you say?" I asked.

"Watch what you're doing," he said again, with an attitude.

Whether it was having to put up with too many mosquitoes or whether I reverted back to my childhood days when I had to protect myself in Woodside, I flipped out. "Don't you ever … Who do you think you're talking to? "… I'll tell you what I'm going to do with this @#^%& car."

"What are you going to do?" he asked.

"I'll drive this #@%&* car into the water if I want to. As a matter of fact, I'm going to do it!" I said. I floored the gas pedal and headed right for the ocean waves.

"What are you doing? Calm down!" Ray said.

As we hit the small waves, I forcibly braked and stopped the car. "Now, you &%@#$, drive me!" I said angrily and got out.

Jimmy Rogers thought this whole drama was so funny that he started laughing from the back seat. He couldn't believe that I was doing this to Ray Downey. To further clarify the reputation Ray had established for himself – the men affectionately used to call him "God."

Ray got out from his side and drove us back. He probably couldn't believe I had done this either, but I had my own temper. Once I let off steam, I was okay. That was my introduction to Ray Downey, and his to me.

Culebra was devastated; we found that the chainsaws we had brought were the most valuable tools for hurricanes, as we helped clear the roads of fallen trees and debris, in order for the Navy to bring in water and supplies to the people. We kept checking the island's natural drinking water for contamination because people were getting sick from the stagnant polluted water. Our relief efforts also had us inspecting the buildings that remained, marking an "X" on those we found unsafe. Those were to be demolished.

Those of us who constituted that first team didn't know it, but we were the forerunner of a permanent team from New York City comprised of firefighters, police, and EMS workers that would make up the New York Task Force Team 1 for FEMA.

When we arrived back at Kennedy Airport, there was a big welcoming party for us. Mayor Koch invited our families and us to Gracie Mansion for a dinner party to thank us for the work that we had done to help the victims in Puerto Rico. That was my first official out-of-town disaster relief work.

Two months after we got back from Puerto Rico, I was assigned as a Lieutenant to 102 Truck, and was in my office one day, when my phone rang.

"Al?" a voice said, crisply.

"Yeah," I said.

"It's Ray Downey."

"Hey Ray, how are you doing?"

"Good. Listen. How would you like to come over to Rescue 2?" he asked.

My mouth must have fallen open. I had always wanted to go to Rescue 2 as an officer. "Ray, are you sure?" I asked, wanting to be sure he was serious. I thought that my having taken him for that wild drive into the waves on Culebra might've made him never want to see me again.

"I'm telling you. You want to come over or not?"

"Absolutely, Ray," I said firmly. I knew he didn't have the patience to ask me again.

After accepting his offer, I was transferred over to Rescue 2. He and I became very close, as did our families. I must say that Rescue 2 was the highlight of my career. I was young, and I found myself with other men at this company who were knowledgeable and aggressive at fighting fires and handling emergencies that were extraordinary in nature – men like Lt. Artie Connelly, Lt. John Viggiano, Lee Ielpi, Pete Bondy, Lou Valentino, Timothy Higgins, Lt. Pete Lund, Mike Esposito, Ed Rall, Pete Martin and Billy Lake, and again, the list goes on and on. These men and the newly assigned ones had all the qualities that characterize firefighters in this city and throughout the world; I learned much from working with them.

While at Rescue 2, Ray continued to build the nucleus of the New York Task Force Team, the emergency response team that would become part of the FEMA (Federal Emergency Management Agency) National teams. In the near future, we would respond to the Oklahoma City Bombing.

CHAPTER NINE

THE MARINE DIVISION

Capt. F: … to the Rescue Battalion …

Dispatcher: Everybody, stand by, unless urgent.

Capt. F: … urgent …

D: Go ahead urgent …

Capt. F: I'm trapped here… it's from the previous
                collapse. I need some help to get out, K …

D: All right. Are you at the west side of the World
                Trade Center? Building Number One in the
                street?

Capt. F: In the rear side of Building Number One …

D: All right. Ten-four. Units that are responding in
                to assist, the trapped members are now
                reported to be in the rear of Tower Number

One, rear of Tower Number One. All units
responding in to assist members who
are trapped to rear of Tower Number One.
Calling car Division Six.

*   *   *   *

While at Rescue 2, I realized that since the F.D.N.Y. and firefighting were going to be my lifelong career, I should continue studying for further career promotions. It was with this thought in mind that I began studying again for the rank of Captain. After passing the test and being on the Captain's promotional list for a short while, I was officially promoted. This meant that I would be leaving Rescue 2. I can't overstate how wonderful those five years were and how fortunate I was to have been an officer in that very special company. The men, the memories and the borough of Brooklyn itself made leaving extremely difficult. My objective was to return to Rescue 2 one day – I hoped – as the company commander.

During this time, the Fire Commissioner had created a Captain's Management Program with the purpose of having newly promoted captains work at and learn higher mid-management skills. A captain would be assigned to work with a chief in any one of the various departments or bureaus.

Battalion Chief Craig Shelley, who previously had been a firefighter in Rescue 2, was the Marine Division chief. He had requested an executive officer and it seemed logical for me to perform my Captain's Management Program in this division. The job sounded interesting, and since I'd been a land firefighter for over twenty years, I took it as another learning experience. Now, I would be looking at the marine aspect of firefighting. I took Craig up on his offer and became his Executive Officer.

In between these career changes, Ray Downey called, and I went with him to another hurricane disaster, this one in the Dominican Republic. It seemed just a short time after that, that Craig decided to retire. In the next two years, there were some different chiefs who assumed the position of Marine Chief. In the meantime, I was asked to fill in as the temporary Captain of Rescue 4, in Queens, a position I accepted.

When I was at Rescue 4 only a week, Pete Ganci called me up. "Al, another chief at the Marine Division just left. I'd like you to come back and stay there for a while, in order to help out, until we can get someone to fill the spot. Give me a hand; we'll work it out."

That was good enough for me. "Whatever you want, Pete," I said.

"Fine. I'm putting you back in as Acting Chief."

The Marine position didn't have me actively involved in firefighting; it entailed managerial, supervisory work. I would be in charge, however, of the firefighting and emergency work in the New York Harbor. I would work four days a week, in ten hour shifts, but again, always on call twenty-four/seven for emergencies or fires.

Ray Downey had already been promoted to Battalion Chief and was presently in charge of S.O.C., Special Operations Command. This put him in charge of all the Rescue companies, the Squad companies, the Marine Division, the rescue school and various other tactical support units. When I heard that Jay Fishler, at the time, the present Captain in Rescue 2 was soon to be promoted to the rank of Battalion Chief, I started dreaming again. I waited in the Marine Division for two years for the position at Rescue 2 to open up. When it did, I applied. That's when I received a call from the then Fire Commissioner Thomas Von Essen, to report to headquarters to see him.

"Al, I want to talk to you," he said. "I hear that you're interested in Rescue 2."

"Yes, I am," I told him.

"Well, there are a lot of Captains requesting transfer into that company. I don't have to tell you. I'm down to two. You and Phil Ruvolo."

"All right."

"I'm going to give it to Phil," he said. "I can't give it to you."

That hurt. I had known Phil for a few years. He was a friend, a competent, good and knowledgeable officer who would make a good captain for the company, but now we were fighting for the same spot. There are always politics involved in getting assigned to some of these positions, especially ones with a profile as high as a Rescue. I wasn't going to learn the whole story that day, so I asked him if I could speak my mind.

"Yes, go ahead," he said politely.

"As you well know," I told him, "I have no weight, no 'pull' to have someone higher up help me get assigned. I came into the Department on my own and worked my way up. Rescue 2's been my dream, and nobody deserves that company more than I do. I've lived for it. I'm qualified and I'm trained for it. You know that, and if you want to know how I feel, I'm angry."

"Well Al, I'm sorry, but that's the way it's going to be," he said. "Can you stay at the Marine Division and help me run it? You'll get another Rescue Company, when one opens up. In the meantime, the Marine Division needs help. Can you help me get that together?"

I was aware it needed a great deal of help. "You're the boss, and I'm only a soldier," I replied. "If that's what I have to do, I will."

The Commissioner had been a firefighter, one of the rank-

and-file, but also the President of the Firefighters' Union, the UFA. When asked by the mayor to become commissioner, Von Essen eagerly accepted and gave up both jobs. No other fire-fighter I know of had ever been asked to fill such a position, or if asked, ever accepted such a position. For whatever reason – politics, I suppose – Von Essen did. I found it ironic that this same commissioner now wanted the Captains in the department to receive "mid-management experience" before they could qualify to be promoted to a higher rank.

I left headquarters that day with emptiness in my stomach, as I realized that with my time on the job, the possibilities of my returning to a Rescue company as a company commander were zero. Other changes took place within the Marine Division, but when 9/11 came, I was once again the Acting Battalion Chief.

CHAPTER TEN

A FIREFIGHTER'S FAMILY

D: Car four-Adam has a command post at …

Capt. F: …unintelligible…

D: Rescue, go ahead.

Capt. F: …we need a couple of guys to lift this beam
              off, K … so we can get out … K …

D: You have help on the way. Do you receive that?
              There is help on the way.

Capt. F: …static …

D: Calling Ladder one-five members … Calling
              any unit that is responding to assist trapped
              firefighters …

                    *   *   *   *

Back in Woodside, as my friends and I became older, we decided to branch out and meet girls from other places; besides, sunbathing on our rooftops, which we called "Tar Beach," wasn't much fun. The 'in' place during the summers was the Hamptons, on Long Island, but the summer rental fees there were so steep that in order to afford a place, about twenty people had to share a unit. If the house had only one bathroom, the place seemed hardly worth the price.

We decided to try Long Beach, a community on the south shore of Long Island, on the Atlantic Ocean. It was a popular spot, and the summer rents were affordable. The first summer worked out perfectly, so we came back for a second. During that stay, my friends and I would try out the many different taverns along Beech Street, the main thoroughfare. One night, an Irish Band, "The Cunningham Brothers" were playing both popular music and Irish, in a bar appropriately named, 'The Sand Bar." I couldn't help but notice a pretty blond girl who was sitting with another. I went over and asked her to dance, and she accepted, or she might have hesitated, but I managed to pull her out of her seat and reassure her with my big smile, that it would be all right. Afterwards, we had a chance to talk, and I learned her name, Eileen Malone. You can't get any more Irish than that! She'd gone out that evening with her friend Tara Clancy, and was on summer break from Hartford University, in Connecticut. That dance led to our dating, which continued while I started my training at the Rock.

I found it ironic that Eileen's father was a successful plumbing contractor in Manhattan. Her mother Catherine, and father Hughie, ran the business together. I remember how her father would always quiz me on plumbing matters, whenever I'd come to pick her up. He was aware that I'd worked in the trade before joining the F.D.N.Y. Although I didn't want to work in the plumbing business full-time, I did help out when they needed someone and when we needed some extra money.

Eileen's mother's desk was the same size as Eileen's father's and her parents sat directly across from one another, equal partners and totally supportive of each other. They were never afraid to shout back and forth, if they disagreed about something, and then after the shouting, they'd act as if nothing had happened and go to lunch together.

The company was a large water main and sewer firm in Manhattan, but it required that they get jobs every day to keep the men working. The real downside to the business was the insurance claims filed against the company. People would claim they'd fallen on a previously dug excavation and were hurt, even five or ten years after the job. Regardless of how safe the conditions were kept, people would fall, purposely.

I found Eileen's parents to be a lovely couple with a wonderful sense of humor, although her mother doesn't realize she's funny. I respected them for all the hard work they put into that demanding business for over twenty-five years. They would get up at five-thirty in the morning and drive from Nassau County into Manhattan, and not get home until eight o'clock every night.

Eileen's parents never expressed a negative thought, feeling or word about my ethnicity. Her parents never made me feel I was 'different,' and my parents never questioned Eileen's background. We were fortunate that both sets of parents were accepting from the start.

Two years after I joined the New York City Fire Department, our good friend Father Deeken married Eileen and me, on December 29th, 1979. Eileen had graduated from the university and had become a teacher. By marrying a firefighter, she was embarking on a course that would be different from that of most of her friends. Firefighters are very family-oriented, but the Fire Department is another 'family' in itself, and the spouses of firefighters understand that this very deep bond to other firefighters runs parallel to the individual family bond.

Our first child was a son, Matthew. Eileen's earliest memory of taking Matt to a firehouse was at a Christmas party. He wasn't able to walk yet, so was still in a baby-walker. The trucks were out on the street and Matt had the whole apparatus floor to himself. He learned he could push with his legs to set his walker flying across the floor, and the firefighters had a grand time giving him a push and sending him back to the other end of the firehouse. Matt squealed with laughter as he flew across the floor.

Eileen and I were blessed with two daughters after Matt, Caitlin and Elizabeth. Catie has said that the first thing she remembers about a firehouse is a stinky rubber smell. Anytime the children were going into the city, I'd park at a firehouse and tell them, "You have to go in and say hello to the firefighters; if they give you something, always say thank you." The firefighters would rub the children's heads and always have candy, lollipops, bagels or soda ready to give them. The children loved going to the firehouses and I loved taking them to see where my brother firefighters and I worked.

When our children were small and I would do a night tour (6 P.M. to 9 A.M.), home-life underwent a transformation. The children would begin by asking their mom, "Is Dad staying over at the firehouse?"

"Yes," Eileen would say.

"I want pancakes!" one would tell her, clearly feeling a new sense of freedom. I would never go for pancakes for dinner. I was used to eating a big meal.

"I want grilled cheese," another one would say.

"And I want cereal," Matt would say. He always ate cereal for dinner, when he could.

It became something of a joke to ask, "Is it one-of-those-nights?" But when they did, Eileen would respond, "Uh-huh. She knew the children would jump for joy, because they could have what they wanted. And the three of them also delighted in being free to eat whenever they wanted to, rather than at a specific time, which I typically required in order for us to have a family meal together. "Yea!" the three of them would yell in delight, and that night at least, they would have their pancakes, grilled cheese sandwich and cereal for dinner.

Although the children had their own perfectly fine bedrooms, on those nights, when I was away, they preferred sleeping with their mom. She would sleep on her side of the bed, with Catie and Liz in bed with her, and Matt would lie across the foot of the bed. They would usually fall asleep there after Eileen had read to them.

Eileen remembers how other firefighters' wives talked about how their husbands would have to sleep after coming home from a night tour. The house would have to be quiet. I'd been blessed with a healthy body and plenty of energy, and never had to pace myself. After a night tour, I'd often go over to Manhattan to work for Eileen's father and after that, I'd return to the firehouse to work another night tour.

One advantage to my schedule was that I could occasionally be with the children during the day. If there was an event at school, I was able to go, while the other fathers were at their more 'normal' jobs. When the children were young, we were concerned - living in Long Beach – about the dangers of the beach and the canal waterways. We wanted to teach Matt, Catie and Lizzy how to swim, so I took them to the Long Beach recreation pool for swimming lessons. The funny thing was that I was the only dad in the children's swimming classes. The instructor would say, "Okay, mothers let's get started, and you too, Dad." We would all sing, "Ring around the rosie, we all fall down," and we had to blow in our babies' faces before dunking them below the water. Eileen was working, and in this way, I was able to help with the children. We were a struggling two-job family, but not a nine-to-five family.

Our children grew up experiencing the richness of three cultures: Irish, Spanish and American. Eileen never promoted one culture at the expense of the other. We traveled to Ireland and visited Glengariff, where the children's great-grandparents were born, but we would also taste Spanish culture when visiting my parents' apartment in Woodside. Christmas Eve, for instance, would be celebrated there. My sisters' and brother's families would join in the celebration. We'd all have a great time, as everyone squeezed into the apartment. Because Eileen's parents celebrated Christmas Day, they would come also. We loved being there to enjoy the Spanish food, Spanish music, the good times with relatives, and our Spanish tradition of exchanging gifts at midnight.

The Fire Department provided yet another experience, and that "Family" would open its arms wide at special times during the year. One of the best times for all the children was the annual Christmas party at the firehouse. A month ahead, I'd come home and announce, "Put the date for the party on the calendar." No matter what else was happening, we wanted to make sure that we made it to the Christmas parties. They were a good way of meeting other firefighters' families and having a wonderful time.

The families would bring presents for their children, each labeled appropriately, and the presents were put right away into a large room. The firefighters would proudly have cooked the whole night before, as well as that morning, and when the wives and children arrived, there would be trays lined up, overflowing with lasagna, chicken, and every conceivable kind of food, for everyone to feast on. The firefighters would already have looked around to see who among them was the chubbiest, and appointed him Santa. We had authentic, expensive Santa outfits, as we took the whole issue of Santa very seriously. Everyone agreed that Santa Claus should appear as authentic as possible.

The children would become so excited when one of the firefighters began calling on the radio, "We have a Santa Claus sighting! Santa is coming!" They'd start yelling, "Santa is coming!" Then the dispatcher would call on the radio, "Santa Claus has just been seen flying around the quarters. I think he may be landing on the roof." Suddenly everyone would hear a Bah-boom, as someone upstairs dropped some iron weights for sound effects. When Santa Claus would appear a few minutes later, the children would go bonkers with joy.

After Santa's arrival, he'd be assisted by a firefighter who would pass the presents; the children would sit around in a circle to wait for their names to be called. Santa would say, "Matt Fuentes, come on up here." Each youngster would go and sit on Santa's lap, and as Santa handed that child a present, another firefighter with a big camera would take a picture. It was fun listening to some of the children ask questions like, "How did Santa Claus know what I wanted? I didn't even send my letter yet."

Some years we added more fun to Santa's arrival when we had him landing on the roof. The children would be taken outside, where they would see Santa "stuck" on the roof. "Santa's stuck! We have to get Santa Claus off the roof with the truck! He's stuck!"

Other adults would shout, "Be careful, Santa!" We might call a nearby company to bring their truck with a Tower Ladder (a cherry picker) to bring Santa Claus down. Santa would climb inside the basket and be brought safely down by the firefighters. When he got out on the street, the children would scream to greet him. It was great fun seeing everybody so happy.

The other big event with our extended family was the company picnic; many of these were held at Mushroom Park, in Lido Beach. The park is so named because tall cement columns climb two stories into the air and are topped with giant 'mushroom' caps that fan out over the tables to protect everyone from the weather.

The picnics included family members, friends, widows, and retirees. The firefighters who enjoyed cooking would start up the grills in the morning and serve breakfast; they'd continue later with hot dogs to hold people over for the main meal, and by evening, put on the hamburgers, sausages, ribs and steaks. They'd prepare different kinds of salads, and because the picnics were meant to be fun for the children, there would also be ice cream, cotton candy and cake. In between all the eating, there were regular events, like pillow-case races, water balloons, an egg-throwing contest and swimming.

Everyone was free to have a wonderful time at the picnics because everybody shared the responsibility of taking care of the children. Our children still remember the names of the girls who helped to watch them, and I remember how Erin, Bobby Burns's daughter, loved to walk the baby carriages; it was such a pleasure to have her help that Eileen once joking-ly asked her mother if she might take her home with her. As our children got older, our girls would love taking their turns watching Ray Downey's granddaughters.

I remember one Rescue 2 picnic especially. After it had ended, we had people come back to our house about a mile or so away, because no one wanted to go home. We had a pool and lived on a canal; the pool was filled with the children swimming, and when they tired of that, they went to the canal or tried crabbing off our old dock. Darlene Rall, wife of firefighter Eddie Rall, had just met us that year, and she always remembers the good times we had, that night among them.

Firefighters and their families enjoy life and have large parties to enjoy the good times together, but we also share some of the saddest. We're on intimate terms with death; it is a recurring theme in all our lives. There's a saying in the department, "We never leave anyone behind," and on the occasions that we're forced to back out of a fire, the significance of this saying becomes clear. If one of us should die in the line of duty, the whole Department takes part in the funeral. Many firefighters who aren't working that day will attend, and this brotherhood extends across the nation. Firefighters from Los Angeles, Boston and Philadelphia will come to New York, and we'll travel to their cities, should they lose a brother. All of these trips are out-of-pocket expenses.

After my good friend, Firefighter Louie Valentino of Rescue Company 2, died in the line of duty in 1996, I became very close to his family. I was one of the firefighters who drove to his house to assist his wife Dianne and his parents. After the funeral, I'd go to Louie's father, Lou Sr., like another son, to chat and seek advice.

Throughout the wake, I stayed in the firehouse and at Louie's house, as did many of the men from Rescue 2, to assist his family in preparations for the funeral, and to anticipate any needs they might have. Eileen knew that I'd be away helping the family and didn't expect me to come back until I felt I had done everything I could. As one of the officers of the company, I wanted to make sure that everything was taken care of.

After waking up at six in the morning, I had a cup of coffee; the men of Rescue 2 were also up and ready to help. I remember saying to Bill Esposito and Danny Murphy, "Get over to the funeral parlor before Louie wakes up."

"What?" they asked, surprised.

"Get over to the funeral parlor before Louie wakes up," I repeated. I wanted somebody standing next to the casket, so that he wouldn't be alone. Other officers and firefighters made their way over to Louie's family's house to get breakfast for them and see who needed to be driven to the funeral home or anywhere else, for that matter. We made sure that everything was worked out and that none of his grieving family lacked for anything. I wasn't on duty when Louie died, but I had the honor of delivering his eulogy.

Lou's family hadn't had too much exposure to the Fire Department until after Louie died. They came to see how we respect our brothers and they came to adore us for our outpouring of love and support. They knew that if we could have, we would have carried Louie to heaven ourselves.

There are commitments and friendships within the department that many people, in their jobs, never get to experience. Years after Louie's death, the Valentino's would remember how Billy Lake used to go to their house and bring bagels from Dunkin' Donuts. "Every week, those guys from Rescue 2 would come in and ask, "Where's Grandma? We brought her some bagels."

Every year, the Valentinos have a memorial mass for Louie. After the mass, Lou, Sr. takes everyone – regardless of how many attend the mass - back to a restaurant in Brooklyn. If there are a hundred people there, they all go to the restaurant, and he pays for the meal, a feast that ranges from soup to nuts.

CHAPTER ELEVEN

RESCUE AND RECOVERY

Marine 9:   M-9 to Manhattan, K …

D: M-9, go ahead …

Marine 9:   …With respect to Marine Battalion's request
                (Captain Fuentes) … we have a rescue…
                qualified officers and firefighters … we'd like
                to be directed to assist the Marine Battalion
                and other …

D: O.K., Marine 9 … continue in … give any
                assistance you can give

Marine 9:   Ten-four

Rescuer: All right urgent … I've got a trapped
                firefighter …

D: Go ahead with your urgent …

Rescuer: Anybody operating on the West Side … on the West Side Highway … I have a member with … alive. I need some help. Anybody that's over here searching with me …

D: All right. Unit … the person calling for help … what ID, K? Identify.

Rescuer: Battalion Chief Fuentes is trapped. I have him. It's Flatley with Rescue… West Side Highway … I need some help getting him out. There's members over here. I have no radio.

D: All right. Ten-four. We do have some units on their way over there to try to assist you. Marine nine should be docking momentarily. They also have rescue personnel on board.

Rack 2:   Rack two … acting Rescue two, second support unit to Manhattan.

D: Rack 2 acting Rescue two support unit.

Acting
Rescue 2:   We have commandeered city buses. We have the tools and equipment, eighteen men, three officers … currently at … Park Row in front of City Hall and moving into the city with members. Please advise the captain of the trapped members on the west side of the World Trade Center.

D: Ten-four. You're responding over there? Ten-four. Rescue 2: there's a direct rescue right now ...

D: Ten-four.

D: All right. Manhattan to the marine battalion... Calling firefighter on the west side, K ...

Rescue 3: Rescue three support units to Manhattan.

D: All right. Manhattan to Marine nine, K. Marine nine ... Rescue Two support is on the way over to the west side to lend assistance ...

Marine 9: Ten-four... to Manhattan... will advise you when we get in. Ten-four.

D: Ten-four. Command post ...

Command
Post: can you have the Mask Service ... backup units respond to ... West and Chambers Streets to the staging area, K?

* * * *

I remained trapped and pinned for over forty-five minutes, while I drifted in and out of consciousness. The once vibrant World Trade Center had become totally isolated, a desolate war zone. Everyone who could had run from the collapse of the towers and the choking clouds of dust; the others had perished in a matter of seconds. An eerie silence followed.

As I radioed the dispatcher, I had started using different identities to get his attention: Captain Fuentes, Marine Division, Marine six, Marine Battalion and Rescue 2. I was losing focus and reverting to my past commands, and I couldn't remember what I was telling him.

After considerable time had passed, I think I surmised that everyone was dead, and that it would be quite a while before others responded. I was in serious pain; I was delirious; I kept thinking, they're not getting to me.

My first rescuers initially heard the noise from my radio transmissions. Unable to see me, they kept hearing the static and the talk until they finally looked into a hole and saw a bit of my fire coat. These firefighters had responded from home as had many others that day, and without waiting for orders, they had begun the grueling task of trying to search for survivors. Thank God they did.

I was gurgling blood, so they knew right away that I had internal injuries and they tried to put paper or whatever material they could find, against my head, where my scalp had been cut away. Once they had me aboard the fireboat, the pilot, Scott Hanson, saw flashing red lights on the Jersey shorefront.

"What are those lights?" he asked.

"That's a triage center," somebody responded.

"Then that's where we're going," he told them.

I don't remember this, but I was telling them that I couldn't lie on my left side.

The fireboat went across at full speed. The Hudson River isn't a mile across, at that point, so it took only a couple of minutes for them to arrive at a rebuilt waterfront pier at the Jersey City shore.

As soon as we reached shore, I started to go into respiratory failure. They immediately gave me oxygen. Doctors and paramedics were all ready to help the victims who might come over. The paramedics started working on me right away. There was still doubt that I would survive, so they called over a priest. As they worked on me, he administered the Last Rites there on the Jersey shorefront.

Once I was somewhat stabilized, they rushed me by ambulance to the Jersey City Medical Center, about three minutes away. The doctors there put me into a drug-induced coma and onto a respirator to keep me calm as they started working on me.

PART TWO
SEPTEMBER 11TH 2001

EILEEN FUENTES

CHAPTER TWELVE

9/11, THE START OF THE UNTHINKABLE

I was working in my classroom on September 11th, when one of the other teachers came to my door out of breath and said, "Come to the library. One of the Twin Towers was hit by a plane!" I ran downstairs and joined the others already huddled around the TV, watching in disbelief. People started talking about the people they knew who worked there, and then we began questioning whether or not any of the children had parents there.

As much as I wanted to stay to watch and listen to the news reporters explain what was happening, I knew I had to get back to prepare for my next class; for my students' sake, I would have to act as if nothing were wrong; between class periods, I would run downstairs to see what was happening. Tension grew as we learned that my friend Mary's daughter's fiancé was working in one of the towers. We stood by her as she tried contacting her daughter.

"Let me call Al's office, and see if he's heard anything. Maybe he can get some kind of updated lists," I said.

Our music teacher and friend, Lauren, had a sister working in the towers that day; she left school immediately after receiving a call from her husband. A couple of people came up to me and asked if I'd heard from Al.

"No, but I'm sure he's fine," I told them. I knew from past experiences that he didn't have time to call me during an emergency. I never considered that he might be in any danger. He'd been hospitalized a few times over the years after fires during which he'd taken in too much smoke or gotten his lungs slightly burnt, but he'd always managed to go right back to work. I felt confident that after more than twenty-five years on the job, he knew how to protect himself in a dangerous situation. Our daughter Caitlin had called me from school, and I'd assured her that they were evacuating the buildings and that the firefighters should be all right. At that point, that's what I believed to be true.

I made the call to Al's office to see if I could get information for Mary, and reached Al's secretary, Kathleen. When I asked for Al, Kathleen told me that he'd already left. "I'm sure he's on the fireboat," she said, and I assumed she was right, that he was on one of the fireboats positioned along the shoreline and had no reason to go directly to the buildings. I was more upset that I couldn't get any information on Mary's daughter's fiancé.

Very quickly, the enormity of the situation became clear. The school at which I work is on Reynolds Channel in Long Beach, and from our windows we could see a large plume of black smoke over downtown Manhattan, in the distance. When Tower Two, the South Tower of the World Trade Center collapsed, I had no idea that Al had just escaped death.

At around 10:25, when I had another chance to break away, I joined a few teachers in the library who were watching the news coverage; it was then that Tower One, the North Tower, collapsed. We witnessed a one-hundred-and-ten-story building crash into a cloud of white smoke and rubble, all within seconds. "Oh my God," people gasped. Everything was gone so fast. We wondered aloud about how many had gotten out. I still imagined that Al was on one of the fireboats doing what had to be done; it had never crossed my mind that he had gone to the remains of the Marriott Hotel after the collapse of the South Tower to assist in the rescue efforts, or that he was now among the missing, somewhere in that massive rubble of steel, concrete, asbestos and dust, fighting for his life.

I remember a conversation Rose Downey and I had, when I visited her later. "This may sound stupid on my part," she said, "but I thought Ray would always be all right."

I told her I didn't think it was stupid at all. "I never really worried about Al," I said. "They were so experienced; they were all extremely knowledgeable firefighters. We just believed they'd make good decisions and that everything would be all right." We'd never had reason to doubt that.

When you're married to a firefighter or to someone who has a dangerous job, it becomes almost second nature to convince yourself that things will be all right; you don't allow yourself negative thoughts. I think I'm very good at controlling my mind that way. Even if I'd thought Al was at the site, I'd never have pictured the Command Post, Ray Downey or Al as vulnerable. None of us had any prior experience with a building disaster of such magnitude, and even those of us at school who had watched the collapse on TV, still didn't have any idea of the massive devastation.

The news coverage was focusing on war, terrorists and more plane attacks. People worried that something else was going to happen and we were all concerned about the safety of our families. I was most worried about my three children and whether they would get home safely.

At the end of the day, we were still busy making sure that

all our students were taken care of, that the bus would take them, or that a parent would come to walk them home. We were in the process of making other arrangements for the children whose parents were stuck somewhere, especially in New York City, which had gone into a lockdown for security reasons. At around three o'clock, I decided to call Al's office again.

"Oh, Eileen," Kathleen said in a strange voice. She sounded reluctant to talk to me.

"What's the matter?" I asked.

"Uh… I'm going to put somebody else on."

"No, no, no. I don't want to speak to anybody else." I was comfortable speaking to her. "Really, I don't want to speak to anyone else, Kathleen, just you. What's wrong?" I asked her.

"Al's in the hospital," she said softly.

I still felt relatively calm as I asked, "What happened?"

"Well … let me put Lieutenant Pete Farrenkoft on."

"All right," I said, relenting.

Pete introduced himself over the phone and said, "Al was hurt, but he's okay. We're in contact with a marine engineer, Paul, who is with him at the hospital."

This was sounding too vague. "What hospital is he in?" I asked, pushing the receiver against my ear, anxious to hear his tone, and trying to anticipate where this was leading.

"He's in the Jersey City Medical Center."

"Can I call the hospital?" I asked.

"Calm down. Don't get yourself worked up. Paul is with him and he said he's fine."

I didn't think I was 'worked up.' I was concerned and I knew I would feel better talking directly to Al. "I realize he's okay, but I'd like to speak to him, or to someone who's taking care of him." I decided I didn't want to speak to the lieutenant anymore. "Please put Kathleen back on."

"Don't worry," Kathleen said right away, when she came back on.

"I'm not really worried, but did you speak directly to Paul?" I asked.

"Eileen, I spoke to him. He has a cell phone," she added.

"Can I call him?" I asked.

She gave me the cell phone number and the hospital's number. I could tell by the sound of her voice that she was very concerned too. I decided to call Jersey City Medical Center first.

"My husband's a firefighter," I began. I thought I might be making too much of an issue by calling about Al, when so many other people had been hurt. "I don't really want to bother you – I know it's hectic – but I believe my husband was admitted today. He was involved with the attacks and the World Trade Center collapses."

"I'll put you through to the Surgical ICU," the hospital receptionist said, very kindly.

While I waited for someone to pick up, I wondered why Al would be in the Surgical ICU, if he were okay. But then I reminded myself that they always try to take extra special care of firefighters, and that that was probably the reason.

"My husband's a firefighter. He was hurt. I just wanted to speak to him if I could, or get a status report or see if he needs anything," I explained to a woman at the other end.

"Okay."

"You're Mrs. Fuentes?" a nurse, coming on the phone, asked. She was speaking very quickly, as if she had no time to talk.

"Yes."

"Okay. He's here. We have him. We're working on him. We're doing the best we can," she said in rapid-fire succession.

"What?" I asked, shocked. "Could you start all over again?"

"We're trying our best, but I have to tell you, his vital signs are not good, and his blood pressure is dropping. You'd better get here."

She hung up the receiver, and a sudden chill went through my body. I sat there stunned. My body started shaking uncontrollably.

"What's wrong? What's wrong?" different teachers asked. They surrounded me, as I tried telling them what I had just been told.

"Are you sure?" people were asking from all sides.

"I don't know what to do," I said. "I don't know what to do." As I kept saying this, I was also telling myself, Think of something. Finally, I remembered I had Paul's cell number. I called and he answered. "Paul," I said frantically, "this is Eileen Fuentes."

"Oh, Hi, Eileen," he said softly.

"I called the hospital and they told me Al's in the Surgical ICU and that his blood pressure is dropping; that he's in critical condition. Are you there with him? I asked.

"Yes," he said, "I'm right here with him."

"How is he?" I asked, trying to stay in control."

"Fine. He's fine," Paul said.

"But they just told me …"

"Nope. Five stitches in the head and he looks good," Paul said, interrupting me.

"Paul, please. I need to know the truth," I told him. "Are you sure?"

"No, I'm telling you the truth. Don't worry about anything."

"All right."

"I'll call you back," he told me.

"Okay," I said, and hung up. I called Kathleen back and told her that I'd spoken to Paul.

"Eileen, he called here and gave us the same report as he gave you. It wouldn't make sense for him to minimize Al's injuries. The hospital must have the wrong person. It really is chaotic," she said, reassuringly.

After I hung up, I didn't know what to think. I remained seated in the faculty room wondering whom to call next.

"How about calling your parents?" "How about calling Al's parents?" "Do you want us to call the Long Beach police department? They can probably get you some information." Everyone was trying to be so helpful; they were concerned and wanted desperately to do something, but I felt over-whelmed, so I asked one of my friends to come out into the hallway with me.

As we walked down the hallway, I started feeling very frightened, and began crying. I broke down in front of her say-ing, "I can't do this. I can't do this."

"What do you mean? You can't do what?" she asked.

"Al can't be dead. I can't do this by myself. I can't do this," I said.

"Don't worry," she reassured me.

"You don't understand. I can't do this alone."

She tried to comfort me, and I began to get control of myself. "I'll be all right. I'm all right," I said, knowing that I couldn't just stand there and cry.

"Maybe it isn't so serious."

"I don't know what's true," I said. I took a few deep breaths, and then Karen, my principal, brought me into her office. I was shaky and on the verge of crying again. Then the phone rang, and when someone said it was my son Matthew calling, I collected myself immediately, took a few more deep breaths and said, "I'm fine. I'll talk to him." That was the best thing that could've happened, because I knew I had to be strong for him. "Hi, Matt," I said.

"I just wanted you to know that a marine engineer from the Fireboats called the house. Daddy's ..." Matt began.

"What did he tell you?" I asked nervously, interrupting him.

Matt repeated exactly what Paul had told me.

How long ago did he call?"

"A few minutes ago." "Mom," he said, "I asked him to please tell me the truth, that I could handle it. What are you going to do?"

"I'm coming home. I'll be there in about ten minutes," I said.

Once I'd spoken to Matt, I felt calm. One of my very good friends, Margaret, offered to drive me home. "And then what will you do?" she asked.

"I'm going to go to Jersey City," I said. "After hearing what that nurse said, I really can't just believe what Paul is telling me. Whatever I have to do to get there, I'll do."

"Do you want me to come with you?" she asked.

I was relieved. "Okay, we'll go together."

Margaret followed me home. Caitlin and Matt were already there. I knew nothing, except Paul's story, so that's what I told the children. I didn't want them to worry about something I wasn't sure of myself, even after the conversation with the ICU nurse. I'd make a decision once I got there.

Al would need a few things, I decided, so I packed t-shirts, shorts, and a few other items for the hospital. I wish I had known the truth. In the meantime, I called our best friends Mike and Lorraine, and told them what had happened.

"Mike's going to come down," Lorraine said.

"No, no, it's not necessary. I'm okay. I'm going to go with Margaret."

"Well, he's already left," Lorraine replied.

After getting off the phone, I told Margaret that Mike was coming and that he'd go with me to Jersey City. I really appreciated her offer, but I thought it might be better to wait for Mike because he'd probably have a better idea about how to get there.

Just knowing that Mike was on his way made me feel good. I knew he'd find a way to help me. In the meantime, I spoke to Lynne Turner, another secretary at the Marine Division. I remembered Al's telling me that our friend, Chief of Department, Pete Ganci always spoke so highly of Lynne. He once told him "she could run the Marine Division herself." She was a good friend of Al's, and I knew she'd be truthful and able to help me.

"I want to get to Jersey City Medical Center," I told her. "I don't want to bother the Fire Department, because I know there's so much going on, and if Al's really not that hurt, I don't want to make a big deal out of this. If they can't help me, I'll get there somehow, but if they can, that's even better," I said anxiously, but still feeling apologetic for bothering her and any of the others during this emergency.

"Don't worry. I'll call you right back," she said.

A few minutes later, she did.

"They didn't think they could take you there; they're extremely busy, but I told them they had to get you there. Originally, they thought they could try to take you by fireboat, but Jimmy Korzkniewski, a retired firefighter, is here, and he'll drive you."

Jimmy "K" as Al always called him was recently retired from the F.D.N.Y. Al had always trusted him as a good firefighter. I thanked Lynne and told her I didn't know how to get to Al's office at the Brooklyn Navy Yard.

"Come to my house," she said, "I'll drive you there."

Before leaving at around 4:30, I told my children, "It's going to be a long night. Don't worry." Matt really wanted to come with me but I asked him to stay with the girls. I just felt safer with him at the house. I wanted them to be together because I knew they would take care of each other. We hugged. I tried to be calm, and promised I'd call them as soon as I had any news.

Mike and I drove away in a rush to the hospital, only to find the streets congested with traffic because the police had set up roadblocks. Traffic was being turned away from Manhattan. Sunrise Highway was at a standstill. As we waited, we talked about the day, the kids, everything except Al. I think it was our way to keep each other calm.

"Do you want to call Paul?" Mike asked me at one point.

"No," I said. I couldn't trust him to tell me the truth, and that would just confuse me even more. I was composed, and I thought it would be better to stay in this calm frame of mind.

When we reached the Belt Parkway, the police were turning traffic away. Mike drove up to the officer and explained our situation, and I told the officer who I was. Fortunately, he let us go ahead; the police obviously trusted us, because they didn't ask for any identification.

We finally arrived at Lynne's home in Brooklyn. She got into her car and we followed her, as she drove the back streets through Brooklyn, because the main roads were blocked with traffic. When we reached the Navy Yard, we got out and met a few fire department people by Al's car. Lynne introduced us to the retired firefighter, Jimmy K.; just before we left, she hugged me hard. I knew she cared about Al, and I knew that she was as afraid as I was. With Lynne, no words were necessary.

I was familiar with the name 'Jimmy K', but I had never met him. Jimmy was one of Al's hand-picked men, a land firefighter who had been detailed one summer for the "Surface Rescue Craft" program. He had suffered a heart attack while fighting a fire one day, and Al was there when Jimmy woke up from his surgery. Although Jimmy had retired before 9/11, he responded to the emergency, to assist in any way he could. Jimmy, Mike and I got into Al's Battalion Chief's car – a dark blue one that resembles the unmarked police cars with the red emergency light on the roof. Jimmy took off, with lights and sirens. There were lanes cleared for emergency vehicles, so we had no traffic in front of us. I don't actually know if we were doing eighty along some streets, but it felt it.

At one point, we had to cross a bridge, which was probably the Manhattan Bridge. There appeared to be only one lane open, and Jimmy seemed to pick up the speed to 100 miles an hour. Mike and I looked at each other and grabbed whatever we could, to hold on. Jimmy was on a mission, determined to do his part.

When we entered lower Manhattan, we saw the smoke rising, and the fires, and the empty space where the towers had been. I remember looking over to my left, as we drove nearer Ground Zero, and seeing the pile of destruction. Mike and I were speechless, overwhelmed by a sight no one could ever have imagined. A terrible caustic odor permeated the air, a smell you didn't want to be around. We were stopped more often in Manhattan, even with the Battalion Chief's car. The police officers would peer in at us and ask where we were going, and then ask to see our badge. Everybody in a moving car was considered suspicious.

What I found strangest was the quiet. I'd never been in the city when there hadn't been people and noise, but now the streets in lower Manhattan were empty. This wasn't the vibrant New York City I had always known, but a ghost town. There wasn't a car moving; there wasn't a person in sight, except for an occasional rescue worker or a figure in fatigues. We could have been in one of those films about the sole survivors after a disaster. I had the eerie feeling that the world had ended.

Before we entered the Holland Tunnel, we had to be checked by the police a final time. They let us go ahead, and Jimmy started speeding through. We were the only car in the tunnel, and I remember thinking, what if the tunnel blows up? We didn't know where the terrorists would strike next or what could happen on the way to the hospital.

CHAPTER THIRTEEN

9/11, EVENING

Jimmy pulled up to the emergency entrance of the Jersey City Medical Center at around 8:45 p.m. I suddenly felt cold and a little shaky. As we entered, I looked into the eyes of the people there, afraid of what I might read in them.

"Upstairs. Surgical ICU," a woman directed us. Somehow, that gave me a slight sense of relief. At least, he was still alive. When we stepped off the elevator, a button on the side wall was pressed and the large doors opened. I was about to enter an ICU for the first time in my life.

Before us were beds with curtains drawn around them. We walked in slowly, and I looked for Al. As we reached the last bed on the left side, we could see a large gathering of doctors and nurses around the bed. At first, I couldn't see Al, but I followed Mike up to the bed and found a spot. The first thing I saw was a doctor suturing Al's scalp. Al's head and face were extremely swollen, and the stitches ran from the front of his forehead, along the side of his head, and around to the back. How many stitches, I wondered; then I saw the tubes and the life-support machines, and the seriousness of Al's condition hit me with a jolt.

Jimmy K, with his take-charge manner, marched right up to the doctors and said, "This is his wife. Please fill her in."

I remember just standing there as I continued to watch the doctor doing the delicate job of suturing. I was so relieved that Al was still alive that I stood there for a long moment, just wanting to take that in – he was alive.

Suddenly, Paul, whom I didn't know, except for our telephone conversation, came over and introduced himself, nervously.

"Paul, thank you for staying with Al," I said. I didn't want to deal with his reason for having misled me, earlier. I was too concerned about Al to give it any more thought, but as Paul walked away, Jimmy K stopped him and had a word. I don't know what was said, but I did see Jimmy gesticulating, and he didn't seem happy. I felt a brief smile come to my face as I realized again how much I liked Jimmy.

The doctors explained that Al had been brought in with his scalp flapped over, and after working all day to get him stabilized, they had finally been able to concentrate on the head wound, cleaning it, bringing the scalp down and finally sewing it back into place. He was unconscious, so there was no way for me to talk to him about what had happened.

Dr. Bower gave us an the overview of Al's injuries: the head injury, the collapsed left lung; the chemical burn to both lungs and the fact that they were filled with the contaminated dust and debris from the site; the nine broken ribs, the broken fingers and hand, and the still as yet undetermined back injuries. Al had come into the hospital and stopped breathing, Dr. Bower said. He had to be intubated and then placed in a drug-induced coma that would allow the physicians to do their work.

This was so much to take in.

"Right now, the lung-airway problem is the primary threat to his life," the doctor said. They planned to scope his lungs to assess the extent of the damage, but they couldn't do that yet.

A patient's survival depends on a number of variables, but one of the most significant is the patient himself. Some people rally and do well, and others aren't able to withstand the trauma, and never rally. We were cautioned to just wait and watch, because it was impossible to predict what might or might not happen over the next few days. "We've listed him in critical condition," the doctor said, solemnly "and we have to go hour by hour, so let's get through the night first."

As I watched Al that night, I knew he was in extreme danger, but for some inexplicable reason, I felt that he was going to be all right. From that point on, I never had any doubt that he would survive.

After Dr. Bower left, Mike and I commiserated and agreed that the doctor hadn't seemed hopeful. Another doctor came in to check on Al, and we spoke to him, and while he said basically the same thing as Dr. Bower had, he presented Al's prognosis in a much more positive way. After we'd absorbed all of the medical information, we began to try to digest the magnitude of the tragedy that was still unfolding.

We sat through the night in the waiting room watching the devastation over and over again, grateful to be able to check on Al, still alive, if barely. While we watched the news, hour after hour, the names of our friends began to appear among those listed as missing or gone. I couldn't even cry. I just felt cold all night. It was the saddest night of my life.

While Mike stayed with Al, I went out past the doors of the ICU, to a small waiting room where I could use the pay phone to call my children and give them a little more information.

"Daddy's okay," I told them. "They had to put him into a drug-induced coma. He's in critical but stable condition." I kept my message simple, wanting to be sure they heard the word 'stable,' so that they wouldn't worry too much. I told them that if they felt they were okay, I was going to stay at the hospital.

My brother and cousins live near our home, and I knew they were available to help the children, if they needed anything. Matthew was nineteen, Caitlin, seventeen, and Elizabeth, thirteen. They said that they were taking care of each other, and that my family had already been over with food, and to check to see if they needed anything.

After that call, I called Al's family in Queens to tell them what I knew and to assure them that I'd keep them informed. I made a couple of calls to friends and other family members, and then knowing that I was expected to be at work the following day, I called my principal to tell her I wouldn't be in. I told everyone that although Al was listed as critical, he was stable. I tried to make things sound much better than they were.

Rumors had already begun to spread. Some were that Al had been found trapped in a car; another, that he had fallen off the fireboat. Compounding the communications problem, the F.D.N.Y. issued a list on 9/12 of those who had died, and Al's name was on it. They corrected that error on 9/13, but some people called the house and said to one of the children, "I hear that your father took a turn for the worst." The children, fortunately, knew better, and simply continued to say that he was hurt, but in stable condition.

Any time a firefighter or policeman is taken to the hospital, the department officials are usually there. In these unusual circumstances, nobody came. City officials were scrambling all day to try to make sure that there wouldn't be another attack. The Fire Department had helped me get to the hospital; that was all I'd needed. Once again, I was just grateful to be there with Al.

Jimmy K is not a sit-down-and-wait kind of person. He was already on the go, but before he left, he said, "I'm going to go through the hospital to see if any other brothers are here." He did just that, and then left to go down to Ground Zero, to assist in the search for his many missing firefighter friends.

After we'd been sitting beside Al for hours, the nurses encouraged us to take a break. "Why don't you go get something to eat?"

"I could really use a cup of coffee," Mike said. "Do you want to get something?"

I didn't want to leave. I had this strange feeling that as long as I stayed, Al would be okay. If something were to happen while I was away, I would never forgive myself. "Why don't you go down by yourself," I suggested.

"No, no, come on down with me," Mike encouraged. "I think he's resting. And we'll be right back."

In the end, Mike and I took the nurses' advice and went downstairs. We found old-fashioned coin-operated coffee machines and got coffee, but after tasting it, judged it to be more like colored water. I was still anxious about having left Al alone, so we carried our weak coffee back upstairs and wound up sitting in the waiting room. We saw the same CNN news report seven or eight times, as we sat up that whole night. We didn't want to change the channel because it was hard enough to take in all the details of what the terrorists had done. Even after having heard the story for the eighth time, we were no closer to comprehending it. That night the news reporter announced that Pete Ganci, the F.D.N.Y. Chief of Department, had been killed. Bill Feehan's name was announced as one of those who had died, and then Ray

Downey was listed among the missing.

"Ray Downey," Mike said. He knew both Pete and Ray as good friends of Al's.

"I'm sure that's wrong," I said, shaking my head. "I'm sure Ray and Pete aren't dead." I wouldn't believe that anything so bad could have happened to the two of them.

Mike gave me a puzzled look, but he didn't argue with me. He could probably tell that I was having trouble accepting so much loss.

Al hung on through the night, but he wasn't doing well. I asked the nurses if the oxygen tubes were working, but they told me not to worry, that he was okay.

People who cared for him that night surrounded Al. The doctors were in and out every hour, checking on him, talking to us and keeping us abreast of any changes in his condition. Mike and I stayed close, but we had to take things hour by hour, as the doctor had said, and just keep praying.

CHAPTER FOURTEEN

ELIZABETH (LIZZY) FUENTES
9/11 MEMORIES

On the morning of 9/11, I was in class when my teachers began getting called down to the principal's office. A couple of the teachers came back crying. We thought that something had happened to one of them. We sat there exchanging puzzled looks and wondering what was wrong.

Although it was a clear, beautiful day, the teachers would not let us go outside after lunch. The students began complaining in hushed voices, "Why won't they let us outside?"

One of the girls near me turned on the radio on her portable CD player and we heard the news that planes had crashed into the World Trade Center and the Pentagon. As we listened, we began repeating to each other, "I can't believe this is happening." Then some parents began picking up their children early. When our teacher realized how worried and full of questions we were, she decided to tell us what really had happened. She said, "This was not an accidental crash. It was a terrorist attack." She asked us not to say anything to anyone because the school didn't want to scare the children who might have parents or relatives working at the Twin Towers.

My friends and I found it almost impossible to believe this could be happening in a city like New York. Although at the time we thought we understood, in reality we had no idea of the magnitude of the tragedy. We had the naïve thought that the rescue workers would search for and rescue everyone. We never imagined how terrible it really was. My friend, whose dad is a firefighter in NYC, was much more worried than I was. Nothing ever had happened to my dad to make me worry about his safety. He always returned home. He was also a member of the Marine Division, and not on a truck, so I thought it was unlikely that he'd be on land near the buildings. I had no idea that this sense of his safety would soon change.

Since I was in a Catholic school, the teachers took all the students into church around 2 P.M. for a prayer service. My friends and I were aware of the importance of our prayers; however, the rest of the students were still totally unaware of the attacks.

Around 3 P.M., I stopped by the office before heading home. Mrs. Littlefield, the secretary, said, "Lizzy, your mom called, and she wants you to go home with Annie." I gave a cheerful, "All right."

I must have mentioned my dad because I remember her saying, "Your dad's on the fireboat. Don't worry. Nothing's going to happen. He's not going to get off the boat."

As we walked to Annie's house, we kept repeating, "I can't believe this is happening. How could this happen to us in America?"

At Annie's house, we turned on the TV immediately. The first thing we saw was the replay of the buildings being hit by the planes and then collapsing. We stared at the TV in disbelief.

"I can't watch this. Turn it off," Annie said. The reality

looked more like a movie, so the size of the disaster didn't sink in. With only news about the attack on the TV, we needed to escape. We decided to take a walk to the store. After a while, we came back to Annie's house, and shortly after, Annie's mom came in with the news that my dad had been taken to the hospital with a collapsed lung and a broken hand.

A few minutes later, my brother Matt picked me up and took me home. That's where things got different. I remember Mom rushing around the house very upset and gathering some of her clothes because she was going straight to the hospital. Uncle Mike came because he was taking her there. I remember her talking to my brother and my sister about going to the hospital. She said, "Don't worry. I'll call you as soon as I get there." After Mom and Uncle Mike left, it was only Matt, Caitie and I.

The news about the attacks seemed to be on the TV forever. We stayed in the den watching in disbelief. So many people were calling to get news about my dad that Matt and Caitie took turns answering the phone. There were so many people involved. We didn't know who of Dad's friends were at the Twin Towers, or what was going on. We began hearing on T.V. that some of Dad's friends were missing, but we thought they were under the rubble and that they would be rescued. They always got out.

Our backyard overlooks Reynolds Channel. It offered a direct view of the Twin Towers and the tall buildings of lower Manhattan in the distance. At dusk, we went into the backyard. The sunset sky had turned into delicate pink. As we looked toward the city, we saw this huge plume of black smoke rising. It was so terribly black.

CHAPTER FIFTEEN

THE DAY AFTER

Mike and I didn't sleep the whole night. We had spent most of it cooped up in the ICU waiting room on its upright vinyl armchairs. There was no couch, and the armrests of the chairs prevented us from improvising a temporary sofa. In the end, we resorted to continually changing positions.

Whenever we went inside to be with Al, we'd tell him, "Don't worry. You're going to be all right." In the beginning, he didn't respond, but the nurses told us he could probably hear us, even if he couldn't communicate.

The following morning, the readings on the monitors had changed, and the doctors didn't like what they were seeing. Dr. Ford told us, "We're not satisfied with the way we have him intubated. We don't feel he's getting enough air. We'd like to perform a tracheotomy and get a direct airway, and that way we can also scope the lungs to see what's going on."

After Dr. Ford had explained Al's condition, and the procedure, the other doctors seemed to be hesitating. I sensed that their indecisiveness derived from the projected timing of the tracheotomy. As the doctors held their meetings, Mike and I held our own, to try to interpret what they'd told us.

As all of this was transpiring, a new doctor came on the floor, and Mike approached him and began talking casually. As it turned out, the man was an Army physician who had attended West Point. Mike's son, whom we affectionately call our nephew, and who calls us 'aunt' and 'uncle,' was graduated from West Point, so Mike and the doctor had that in common, and related well. Over the course of their conversation, Mike happened to tell him that the doctors had been talking about a possible tracheotomy, but seemed undecided now.

The physician excused himself and left for a couple of minutes; when he returned, a decision had been made. The tracheotomy would be performed. While we were discussing the surgery, Al's father and brother Ricky arrived. They had come by subway, by PATH train, and by cab to New Jersey.

Ricky, a veteran of the U.S. Military, was at work as a bus driver at John F. Kennedy Airport in Queens, when he first saw the smoke from Manhattan. He turned on the radio and heard what had happened and made arrangements to go home right away. Like the rest of us earlier that day, he hadn't been too concerned about Al, expecting him to be at the Marine Division in Brooklyn, but he was very concerned about his daughter Giselle who worked in a building next to the World Trade Center.

After arriving home, Ricky called to ask about Al. Matt told him that he wasn't at the World Trade Center and that he wasn't involved. That's what Matt believed at the time, but when Ricky called later to get an update as to whether or not Al was safe, and to learn just where he was, Matt told him, "We found out that he was hurt and taken to the Jersey City Medical Center. He's in stable condition, but Mom is on her way there now."

Ricky then passed the message on to Al's parents in

Woodside. He told them that he couldn't drive to New Jersey because the bridges had been closed to all but emergency vehicles. "Please take me," Al's father, Popi, said; that's when they decided the two of them would find an alternate means of getting to Al. Al's mother would wait at home and visit on another day.

Ricky and Popi had walked off the ICU elevator just as the nurses and doctors were pushing Al onto the elevator. It was an unnerving moment for them, because Al was almost unrecognizable. "You talk to the doctor, and we'll go into the waiting room," Rick said at first, while Al's father listened. They were being courteous and trying not to interfere.

"No, no. You come and listen. This is an important decision, and I want you to hear it," I encouraged.

As Dr. Ford started to talk, I saw Al's father become visibly shaken; yet he managed to stay in control. All of us in our small group agreed with the decision for Al to have the tracheotomy. The four of us then went to the waiting room, where we would wait while the surgery was performed. I began updating Ricky and Popi about Al's condition. Al's father sat there very stoic. It was hard on them. Mike and I had had time to begin to process the extreme danger of Al's condition, but they were just discovering it.

Realizing that he would need time from work to be able to visit Al and to bring Popi to and from the hospital, Ricky called his boss to tell him he'd need a few days off, that his firefighter brother had been seriously hurt at the World Trade Center. When he hung up, he had a slight smile on his face.

"What happened?" I asked.

"They've given me two weeks off," he answered.

We all smiled, because this would give Ricky the chance to take a regular turn at Al's side, as he'd wanted to.

One of the problems a family encounters when a loved

one is in the hospital is the inability to know if something is a crisis or not. Mike and I had begun pacing as we waited to hear news of the how the tracheotomy was proceeding. It was impossible for us to sit still, while Al was in surgery. We didn't speak; we just paced.

I kept checking the clock, impatiently. Al had been in surgery for too long; it was now going on two hours since he'd been taken away for a procedure that was only to have taken forty-five minutes. Right away, I thought something had gone wrong. I returned to the nurses' station to see if I could get any information. A nurse called down, and after she hung up, she said, "He's fine. Everything takes an hour and a half longer than what they say. That's just the way hospitals are."

I let out a relieved sigh.

It took a while longer, but the doctor finally came to us and said that everything had gone well.

The doctors and nurses were very good about explaining everything, every step of the way. The nurses were especially good about explaining what to look for. They constantly warned us about the danger of infection.

After the tracheotomy, Al's condition improved visibly. All the numbers on the monitors improved. When the doctors scoped his lungs, they saw that they weren't as bad as they'd anticipated. The lower sections had been burned, but not as severely as they'd expected. Eventually, he was able to be taken off the ventilator.

When the lungs burn, fluid builds up in them. The nurses began every two hours, to flush out Al's lungs with a suctioning tube. As they suctioned, we would watch as a great deal of black soot came out. Each time they'd insert the suctioning tube into the opening made by the tracheotomy, Al's air would be shut off, and he would look as if he couldn't breathe. When the tube was removed, the air would rush back into his lungs.

We knew that Al had survived the collapse of both buildings, and consequently had been exposed to a heavy concentration of the grayish Ground Zero dust and debris. Having been pinned after the North Tower collapse, he'd been unable to take cover and prevent further exposure to the toxic dust. As the cleaning of his lungs proceeded, we actually saw chunks of debris come out: black soot, dirt, gravel, ground glass, and small rocks which may have been pieces of concrete. All this debris had been coagulating in his lungs.

After each suctioning, they would clean the suctioning tubes.

In time, they began suctioning on an "as needed" basis. "Do you need to be suctioned?" a nurse would ask.

Al would nod. He would wince, hating the temporary inability to breathe, as the tube was inserted, but he seemed to know the suctioning was worth the ordeal.

The ear, nose and throat specialist came by regularly to check on him. He told us that Al's vocal chords were red, swollen and damaged. The vocal chords had been another reason they'd wanted to perform the tracheotomy. The doctors had surmised that the tube that had been inserted in the nose and then traveled down Al's throat to his lungs had been irritating his vocal chords. Shortly after the tracheotomy, they were shocked at how quickly the healing process had begun and how well the chords were responding.

During many of those times that Mike and I would commiserate, we would often come back to the topic of the nurses and the exceptional care each of them provided.

Every patient had his own nurse, but the nurses rotated, so they cared for a different patient each day. A male gunshot patient was in the ICU cubicle next to Al, and although he had no one to visit him, his care was just as thorough as Al's. I continued to be impressed by the nurses the entire time we were there. They were always amiable to our visitors and to me, and they treated Al with such dignity when he was totally incapacitated. When he started having allergic reactions to medications and experienced uncontrollable vomiting, their attitude and tone of voice never changed, never indicated any impatience. Al would give them a look that showed he felt bad about the vomiting, but they would say, "Don't worry, Al. Don't worry. It's okay. You're fine. I'm here for you, Al. Just give us a minute."

Each one was so gentle and kind, and thorough, and although most of them were petite, they were able to lift a 230 pound man onto a gurney, seemingly without effort. And they kept everything immaculate. If anything spilled, they cleaned it up right away. Both the doctors and the nurses wanted everything perfect.

When I'd first arrived, I'd told myself that I'd have to watch everything they did. I was so afraid that they would make a mistake and that Al would be hurt. Clearly, my fears had been unfounded. The Jersey City Medical Center's staff proved to be extraordinarily professional and caring. Later, we would be fortunate enough to experience the same sort of treatment at Montefiore Hospital in the Bronx, where Al would be transferred for further treatment.

Al's father, Popi, is the nicest man anyone could ever meet. He's mild-mannered, sweet and easygoing. He never questions, never has a bad word about anybody, and has never shown any evidence of a bad temper. Over the years, we'd occasionally and lovingly tease Al that he hadn't inherited any of Popi's traits. Al's condition was a challenge. Because Al couldn't converse, we were encouraging people to openly express their feelings through touch. Al's two sisters, demonstrative by nature, were always ready to kiss and hug him; they were so loving and caring.

But there was also one special moment when Popi came beside Al's bed. Al had put his hand up, as he'd probably recognized his father. He'd meant to reach out to him. "Come on, Popi, hold his hand," Ricky and I encouraged, but Popi was so nervous. Being with his critically ill son was hard for him. He didn't want to cry in front of him, and his anguish was evident. Suddenly, instead of taking Al's hand, Popi bent down and kissed him. It was a very sweet moment.

A nurse entered and informed me that I had a phone call from a Dr. Prezant.

"Who's Dr. Prezant?" I asked her.

"He's not from this hospital," she told me, as I took the receiver and said hello.

"Hello, Mrs. Fuentes, this is Dr. Prezant. I'm the Fire Department's doctor," he said, introducing himself.

He actually held the title of Deputy Director, the second in command under Dr. Kelly, who was the Director and in charge of the F.D.N.Y. Bureau of Health Services.

Dr. Prezant began by telling me that he wanted me to transfer Al to Montefiore Hospital, in the Bronx.

It was difficult to know whom to trust, and what kind of decisions to make in terms of Al's medical care. Jersey City Medical Center, at the time, might not have had the most stellar reputation, but I was acting on intuition and even more, on everything I had witnessed up to that point. The staff at JCMC had saved Al's life, and the care he was receiving was excellent; I wasn't ready to just move him to another hospital, about which I knew nothing.

My first priority was Al's health. Regardless of any doctor's suggestions about moving him, I had to worry about what was good for him. I felt a certain appreciation for, and indebtedness to, the doctors and nurses in the ICU. A sudden move could prove to be damaging, and could also be perceived as an insult by the very people who had been giving him such wonderful care. My heart began beating faster, as I grew concerned about what to do.

"Listen, I'm going to be totally honest with you, and I want you to be totally honest with me," I told Dr. Prezant. "Whatever you find out about Al's care, whether good or bad, I want to know the truth. If there's a problem, I want to know everything."

"I promise you," he said. "Not that I wouldn't tell you the truth. I guarantee you that whatever you hear from me will be straight and completely honest."

As he talked about the hospitals and the fire department, I tried to keep matter-of-fact and calm, but I finally had to interrupt him. "I said that we were going to be honest with each other from the start, and I don't know if you'll be insulted by this, but I don't want my husband to be a political pawn between Jersey and New York. If that's coming into play here, then I have a real problem with it. I don't want to hear that later. I want you to be Al's doctor, not the Fire Department's."

"Of course, Al would be my priority," he said.

I just felt that it wasn't right to move Al at that point. It was understandable that the Department would want its city firefighters in a New York hospital; on the other hand, I remember how Al would sometimes complain about some of the Fire-Department physicians. I mustered my courage and told Dr. Prezant that I thought it was too dangerous to move Al. That must have frustrated him, because he probably felt he should make the final medical decisions.

"I'm going to come over to the hospital," he responded.

And that afternoon, of September 12th, he did and made a thorough check. After he finished meeting with the other doctors, he met me in the waiting room.

"I have to tell you, I'm really impressed," he said. "I

expected to come over here and say 'we're taking Al out of here.' I was sure I was going to have to convince you to do that, but he's staying. He's too critical, and we'd be taking a chance moving him. I want him to be stable before we do anything."

"I agree," I said, relieved. Although I'm not a doctor, I truly felt that this ICU was topnotch. I was comforted by Dr. Prezant's comments and relieved by his honesty. He would prove to be a true professional, and a friend. He still maintains contact and advises Al on his many injuries.

After we'd made the decision to stay, the president of the hospital came down and thanked me for keeping Al there. I didn't realize how important it was to the hospital. It was important to me to let them know that I felt they had done a good job.

CHAPTER SIXTEEN

MATTHEW FUENTES, AGE 19

Jimmy K drove my sisters and me over to Jersey City Medical Center to visit Dad for a few hours. When the two automatic doors opened, there was a noticeable smell of medicine and bodies, which reminded me right away that I do not like hospitals. We walked through. It was scary being in the Intensive Care Unit.

Mom greeted us. "Dad looks a lot better," she said. But to prepare us for the fact that he was not sitting up in bed and that he was far from his normal self, she turned to Lizzy and said, "He looks like your friend Elizabeth Ryan, who was sick with cancer. He's on medication." Then she took us over to Dad. He looked horrible. His face and neck were very swollen. I could hear his breathing, and the sound of the mucus, from the tracheotomy. There were tubes everywhere. His eyes were open, but I don't think he realized I was there or what was going on.

"Hi, Dad. We're here with you," I said.

He floated in and out of awareness. His eyes showed no sign of recognition, when I spoke to him. I look up to him so much, that to see him in that condition was frightening. I had gone in there with the attitude that I was the brother and the oldest, and I felt a responsibility to set the example for everybody. My dad was right there. I didn't want him to see me break down. I wanted to let him see that I thought he was going to make it. I wanted to give him positive feelings, and maybe he would recover faster.

While standing there, I felt my sister Caitlin leaning heavily against my back. As I turned to tell her to move a little, she collapsed to the floor. Elizabeth saw her faint and began crying uncontrollably. The nurses came over and asked Caitlin if she were all right. Once she sat in a chair, she felt a little better and wanted to stay. As Caitlin began to get her color back, Elizabeth stopped crying. The three of us had just been shocked to see Dad so distorted and in such bad shape.

When I took a break, I found there were newborn babies in the maternity ward across from the ICU. Occasionally, I would leave Dad and go look at the babies for a while. It seemed ironic to be looking at newborns, while across the hall my dad was struggling to live.

*　*　*　*

Ray Downey and Jonathan Ielpi, Lee Ielpi's son, also a firefighter, were listed as missing. When we'd first met with Mom in the hospital, she told the three of us that she really wanted to be able to talk to Ray's and Lee's families. She didn't want to write them a letter, because that wouldn't be personal enough. "I can't leave and go see them, but I wish someone could. Do you feel you could do that?" she asked us.

"Of course, let's do it," my sisters and I agreed eagerly. We started planning with Mom that we would get three yellow mums with red, white and blue ribbons. We chose yellow because yellow signifies hope. A feeling came over me, that I was the lucky one because Dad was still alive, and that we should be worrying about those people who had only a little hope to cling to.

Jimmy K drove us to Lee Ielpi's house first, but we were told that he and his wife were over at a bridge in town that had been turned into a makeshift memorial for Jonathan. My sisters and I made our way over there, each of us carrying a yellow mum. Lee's wife Anne was on the bridge, and people were signing placards which had been placed there to honor the firefighters and those missing. We gave our flowers, and I said a couple of prayers. A quotation from Victor Frankel, a concentration camp survivor, came to mind, "…only through suffering can you find how beautiful life is." I looked beyond the bridge and saw the sun, and I realized once again that I was the lucky one. All I could do was try to give the others hope. There is no describing the great sadness we shared, and yet joy in being able to hug one another.

We left Anne to continue on our way and deliver our remaining flowers to Ray Downey's wife, Rose. On the ride over, we began talking about how we were going to act in front of Ray's family. It had only been a couple of days since 9/11, so the family was clinging to their last thread of hope that Ray would be found alive.

When we got to the house, there were friends and family outside, and we met Ray's daughters, Marie and Kathy. Ray's three sons Joe, Chuckie (both firefighters) and Ray, a teacher, were at Ground Zero, searching for their dad. Marie and Kathy talked to us a little; we began reminiscing about old times like the Christmas parties and the picnics. After that, we told them that we'd like to talk to their mother.

Marie excused herself and went to tell Rose that we were there. Before this, Rose had told her daughters that she didn't want to see anyone, but Marie came back to say, "I told her the Fuentes kids are here, and she said to tell you to come in."

As Marie took us upstairs, we explained that we didn't want to bother anyone. She showed us to a small room. The door was closed, and when we opened it, we saw Rose sitting on the couch with a blanket, holding her rosary beads. She was clinging to them. I looked at her face that had a look of hopelessness; her eyes were red from crying.

The first thing that came out of my mouth was, "You just have to have hope. You've got to keep praying and hoping. All our prayers are with you. We're hoping too. My mom wishes she could be here with you, but no matter what, we're here, and we're praying."

"Yes," Rose said.

We each gave her our mums then.

"Thank you so much," she kept repeating. After putting the flowers down, we exchanged hugs and kisses with her.

On the way home, having seen what had transpired, Jimmy K became overwhelmed. I'm sure he was hurting also. He started crying, saying what great kids we were for bringing the flowers to the Ielpi's and to Rose Downey. "I'm going to tell your dad when he wakes up, how wonderful you kids were today. He would be so proud."

We were just doing our small part to help those who were hurting. I still remember Rose holding our hands and looking into our eyes. She was heartbroken thinking Ray was never coming home.

CHAPTER SEVENTEEN

KEEPING AL ALIVE

Al began to have lucid moments. Because of the tubes inserted into his throat, he couldn't speak. In order to communicate, he would use a combination of gestures and sounds.

"Where am I?" he'd gesture.

"Jersey," I'd reply.

Then he would give this puzzled look as if to say, "Why am I in Jersey?"

Sometimes, he would try to write. One note asked, "How many brothers?"

I tried to determine what he remembered, and then move gradually from there. "You remember that the tower collapsed?" I asked.

He nodded, but looked unsure.

"Do you remember anything else?" I asked. "The first tower collapsed, right?"

He nodded slightly.

I tried saying something else about the situation to test how much he knew.

"Ray?" he wrote.

"You were with Ray," I said.

Al hesitated and nodded.

I looked at Mike. "I don't think he knows about the second tower collapsing."

I had a strong sense that he wasn't aware of the scope of what had happened, and based on the doctor's recommendation, we'd made the decision not to tell him about all the people who were missing, or those confirmed dead.

We observed that there were certain things that he was keenly alert to, while others he seemed unaware of. One of the first notes he wrote to the nurses was to tell them that he was allergic to aspirin. He also wrote the words, "My prognosis?"

I was pleasantly surprised. Oh my, I thought, he's got pretty good thinking skills. He spelled the word prognosis correctly.

The notes Al wrote told me that he was coming back. There were other signs as well. Al was accustomed to being in charge. Now, he kept worrying, trying to ask me questions in spite of his drifting in and out of consciousness. At times, he was more alert, and at those times, he would become agitated. I finally figured out that he wanted to know who was in charge at the Marine Division.

"Don't worry. Bill Guido is there," I kept reassuring him. Bill was the retired Deputy Chief who had come back to volunteer to help the Marine Division during the crisis. Bill is another example of the kind of people the F.D.N.Y. is so fortunate to have, but doesn't always appreciate. Al kept writing on his tablet, "Bill Guido," insisting that Bill come to the hospital.

I called Bill and asked him to drop by for a few minutes.

He did, and he seemed nervous, as if he expected Al to ask him some sensitive questions to which he shouldn't provide the answers, since they might provide information that Al still wasn't to be made aware of.

I tried calming Bill by saying, "He's not going to grill you. He doesn't remember everything. It'll just give him reassurance to see you."

When I brought Bill over to Al's bed, Al was obviously not fully alert.

"Just tell him not to worry, that everything's fine. Say something to make him feel somewhat briefed," I whispered to Bill.

"Al, it's Bill," he said, as he leaned towards Al.

Al looked up at him, either trying to focus his eyes or to remember who Bill was.

"Don't worry, Al. We've got the water coming. We're putting the fire out at Ground Zero," Bill explained. I was sure that put Al at ease, for the time being.

Al stared back. After hearing a few sentences from Bill, Al's eyes would roll.

Bill was still talking when I nudged him and said, "That's good, Bill. He'll probably go to sleep now."

I escorted him out to the elevator and thanked him for coming. Although there was no conversation between them, I hoped Al could rest better knowing that his friend Bill was doing what he could to help the situation. Some things Al remembered, some he didn't; later, he didn't remember this visit. Still, every lucid moment he had gave me hope.

Ricky asked if I would mind if he brought his digital camera to the hospital, to take pictures of Al. "I want to document what these people (the terrorists) did to my brother," he said. He would also keep his relatives in Ecuador informed about Al's condition by sending the photos as attachments to his e-mails.

With the improvement in Al's breathing after the tracheotomy and each suctioning, I felt reassured that he was making progress in his recovery. I told Ricky that I'd like to go home for an hour. "I just want to grab some clothes and see the kids. But I'd really like someone in the family to stay. Are you able to?" It was about four o'clock in the afternoon. He was, so we arranged for Mike, Ricky and Popi to stay with Al; meanwhile, Al's sister Elizabeth, and my sister Kathy also came by, so Al had plenty of family members to stay with him.

Jimmy K came over to the hospital, picked me up, and we were off for another fast ride to Long Beach. When I got home, Jimmy talked to the children, while I took a shower and then came down to talk with them. I was worried about them, but I knew I had to get back to Al; I think they understood. At that point, I had had no sleep and was running on adrenaline alone. Before I left, I packed one change of clothes in an overnight case, since there was no place for me to store my clothes in the hospital.

When I got back to the hospital, we decided that Mike and Lorraine would rotate their turns staying with me. If Mike stayed through the night, Lorraine would be there with me through the day. "If you need anything or want anything, just call us and we'll drive past the house, and bring you what you need," they reassured me. Lorraine also offered to run to the store whenever I needed anything.

Mike and Lorraine are our very closest friends. They stayed and helped me stay balanced through the stresses and anxieties. When I didn't want to talk to anyone about questions that would arise or uneasy feelings, I would turn to them. I needed them to be there, to talk to and give me their support. I appreciated their presence, even during those times that we just sat together quietly without saying a word. They made everything easier for me; I couldn't ask for better friends.

On the third night, the staff was kind enough to offer me an empty room two floors above, where I could sleep in a bed. I had had no real sleep since getting up to go to work on the morning of 9/11. My world had changed incredibly in one day. I knew that if I didn't get sleep, I would collapse.

"Okay, I should sleep," I agreed, reluctantly accepting the offer. Then I turned to Mike and said, "Mike, if I'm going to sleep, why don't you go home. Let Ricky stay with Al, and you get a little break, too." By now, the F.D.N.Y. had detailed two men from the Marine Division to assist us. Instead of their working at the Division, they would split their work time assisting our family, driving or helping with other things that needed to be done.

F.D.N.Y. Marine Pilot Scott Hanson and firefighter Tommy Woska, the two men detailed, did so much for us. When Mike agreed to take a break, Tommy Wosca gave him a quick ride home, while Ricky kept watch at Al's bedside. Scott kept the schedules for us and made sure we all ate and were comfortable.

The hospital had also arranged for me to shower on another floor, which turned out to be an entire unused maternity ward. Before showering, I had to call to make arrangements for someone to accompany me and wait outside, for security reasons. When I arrived on the ward, I found myself having the luxury of showering in a beautiful maternity suite. What joy it was to relax under the warm water pelting my muscles that had been so tense and stressed throughout the whole ordeal.

Security was a very real issue though, especially for a lone woman showering on an unoccupied ward in a big city hospital. The staff was very accommodating about the shower, but ultimately, I felt pressure not to linger in the comforting water too long. The person waiting for me had to get back to work.

When I reached the empty room and settled into bed, I fell asleep as soon as my head rested on the small pillow. I fell into a deep sleep where I had no worries, no anxieties. Suddenly, I was jolted awake by a clanging sound. I sat up, wondering if it were a fire alarm. But if there were a fire, what would happen to Al? He was two floors below me. How would we get him out? I jumped out of bed and took about three steps to find myself in the hallway. I saw the nurses sitting at their station, and headed for them.

"That's a fire alarm. What's going on?" I asked, straining to talk over the alarm and make sense of what was happening.

"Oh, don't worry about it," one nurse replied casually.

Don't worry about it? Where's the fire? My husband's on the third floor; I'm on the fifth. How are we going to get out, I wondered, in my sleep-deprived, half-awake brain. " I have to get to my husband. What can I do?" I asked.

"You can go down on the elevator," she said.

"All right," I agreed, not even awake enough to tell her that you're not supposed to use elevators during a fire. I walked down the hallway to the elevator in my sweats that I had slept in, just in case something was happening to Al.

When the elevator door opened, I got on and pushed the button for the third floor. The elevator stopped, and I got off. The doors closed behind me. I knew that all I had to do to get to Al was to go through the doors. He was just on the other side, but when I pushed the door handle, nothing happened. The hallway doors had automatically locked when the fire alarm went off, and now I was locked between the elevator and the ICU doors. I started thinking that if there was a fire, I was going to die here in this little space. I was half-asleep, stuck, and still hearing this clanging bell on the other side of the doors, so I decided to take another chance and get back on the elevator. By the time I reached the fifth floor and the nurses' station, I felt very disturbed.

"What happened?" a nurse asked.

"I got locked out of the ICU. I don't want to stay on the fifth floor; I don't want that room. I want to go back," I said, almost in tears.

"All right, I'll take you down some other way," she said, obviously feeling sorry for me.

Once I got back to the ICU, I found that Al was resting. I decided to go to the ICU waiting room, where I pulled two of the upright vinyl chairs together. I thought that if I could just get comfortable, I'd be okay. With the two chairs squeezed together, I curled my body up as small as possible and found a way to rest my head, and I managed to fall asleep that way.

I was wound so tight, worrying about Al. I worried about how vulnerable he was, how he couldn't care for himself, and I felt it my responsibility to be with him as much as possible, to make sure he was getting the proper care every second. I only wanted a little sleep. I never went back to the fifth floor.

CHAPTER EIGHTEEN

JERSEY CITY MEDICAL CENTER

Al was still struggling to stay alive. His mother came on Friday, and as we walked into the ICU towards Al's bed, I was nervous. I wasn't sure of how she was going to react when she saw him all swollen and bruised and on life-support machines; I could see that she was struggling to hold back tears. Watching her trying so hard to be strong made my heart hurt. And yet, she seemed instinctively to know what to do.

Very softly, she began talking to him. I stepped back a little as she started to tenderly massage his hands and stroke his face. Her hands and voice seemed so sure and soothing. Her presence seemed so important, but somehow, it was also disconcerting for me, because watching her comfort him made him appear so much more vulnerable. This was her child, her boy, and she might lose him. This could be Matt, I thought, and for the first time, I saw Al through her eyes, and suddenly everything became terribly real and frightening.

I felt deep love for her, as I watched her with her son that day. When I look back, I realize that something very special happened between us that would change our relationship forever, and I'm eternally grateful for that. She came again on Saturday, and then pretty much every day that she could, while Ricky and Al's father came together every day, day and night.

What I most appreciated about Al's parents, sisters and brother was how supportive of me they all were. They made it easy. They helped me when I asked for help, and put no pressure on me. They had no expectations of me; instead, they made me feel strong and sure of myself. One day in the waiting room, Al's sister Liz came and sat beside me; I was so surprised when she suddenly started telling me how much she appreciated how much I loved Al. She actually thanked me for loving her brother so much. I was so overwhelmed that I didn't know what to say to her. I don't think she knew how much it meant to me; to this day, I consider it one of the nicest things anyone has ever said to me.

After he'd been in the hospital for about a week, Al began developing some strange behavior. "What's wrong with him?" I finally asked a nurse, because this wasn't the Al I knew.

"He's got ICU psychosis," the nurse said.

"Psychosis?" I asked, slightly alarmed.

"It goes away as soon as a patient gets out of the ICU," she said soothingly. "Don't worry."

Patients who must remain in ICU for any length of time can become psychotic. The medical staff explained that the psychosis develops as a result of the noise of the machinery and the lack of being in touch with the outside world. The patient becomes paranoiac, thinking everyone is out to get him, and will do anything to get out of the Unit.

In spite of the dangers, the situation can also be a little humorous. You see the patient trying to be tricky, placing one foot out of the bed and looking to see if anyone notices. He resembles a child trying to see if he can get away with something, under the noses of the adults. While they occasionally felt frustrated by Al's behavior, the nurses never raised their voices. He did fall a few times, so his actions could have had serious consequences, but they would simply gather to help him back into bed. The situation was complicated because Al was able to see the bathroom door and he wanted desperately to be able to use the bathroom on his own. They finally had an orderly sit at the end of his bed to watch him. And Al began sending me notes that read, "Get me out of this place."

At one point we were encouraged to bring in pictures to try to help Al overcome the psychosis. They thought pictures of home, family and friends might help bring him back to reality. Whenever pictures and cards were brought in, the nurses brought out the scotch tape and helped to hang everything up on the walls. We had pictures of Al and Louie Valentino, his deceased firefighter friend from Rescue 2, and pictures of the rest of us. And of course, we hung a huge American flag right where Al could look at it every day.

Two months prior to 9/11, we'd had a birthday party for Mike and Al who were both turning fifty within a month of each other. For that occasion, we'd had a DJ, old friends and all the relatives. Al's brother had taken digital pictures of the party and had them on the computer. Ricky went to the trouble of making a beautiful collage of those pictures and mounting it onto on a large piece of cardboard to help comfort Al. I'm sure it helped.

So many people shared their gifts with us. Mike Razzoli, a firefighter from the Jersey City Fire Department came to the Jersey City Medical Center Emergency Room as soon as he'd heard that a critically injured firefighter had been brought in. He was with Al during those first few hours before any of us had arrived. As soon as he heard I was staying at JCMC, he offered his help, and we took an immediate liking to one another. A few years earlier, Mike had suffered a very serious injury to his lungs, so he had some idea of what we were struggling with. He became our lifeline in Jersey. Every day he would visit and bring us food. He'd gone around to the restaurants in the community and explained our situation.

The restaurants were extremely kind and donated enough food to feed an army. The outpouring of love and support from the Jersey City community was overwhelming. Two local Italian restaurants delivered their delicious food to us almost every night. The local firehouses prepared meals for us and personally delivered them to the ICU waiting room. We never had to ask. It was something that Mike Razzoli arranged. The local restaurants responded out of their hearts to show their support after 9/11.

Mike Razzoli treated us like family; I'd known him for only a few days, and I trusted him completely. To this day, he frequently calls inquiring about Al, the rest of the family and our friends. We consider ourselves extremely lucky to have him as a friend.

I began questioning myself again about when to tell Al about the entire scope of the tragedy. He still wasn't aware that many of his close friends had died. I decided to ask Dr. Prezant for advice, and he didn't hesitate with his response. "I don't want him to know anything. He's in no state to handle any kind of shock. He's aware of how horrible the collapse was, but he's not ready to handle any further distressing information about his brothers." I knew that I would wait.

As the days wore on, the media began to gather information about Al. They made it known to the hospital and to the Fire Department that they wanted to conduct an interview. Of course Al wasn't in any condition to talk; he was barely conscious. And I wasn't comfortable talking to anyone at that point. Too many others had lost loved ones; that was who the media should be focusing on, I thought.

A few days after 9/11, we heard that President Bush was coming to Ground Zero. I was told that his helicopter was landing in Jersey City, and that he would proceed from there to Ground Zero. Given the fact that there were injured rescuers in JCMC, he might also want to stop by and visit Al and the family. I remember responding very quickly, that I really didn't want anyone to come. "He's the President of the United States. Is it politics?" they asked.

Of course, it wasn't politics. It was fear. I had spent time in the ICU waiting room watching all the TV talk about more possible terrorist attacks. Miraculously, Al had survived both collapses. I wasn't taking any chances. The terrorists could try blowing up Jersey City Medical Center, if President Bush were here.

It seems kind of silly now to have worried about the hospital's being blown up, but at the time, anything seemed possible. I didn't need the confusion of the cameras; besides, Al was too drugged to know what would be happening. "Please understand. I just don't want that worry," I finally said.

The President never did come that day. I don't think we were ever really a part of his actual plans, but if we had been, I hope that someone graciously told him that Al was too sick to see him. That was the truth.

CHAPTER NINETEEN

THE MOTORCADE –
PASSING GROUND ZERO

While Al was still conscious only sporadically, the times that he was, he was alert enough to answer questions by nodding yes or no. I took the opportunity to ask him if he knew Dr. Prezant. He nodded. "Good or bad?" I asked, and he gave me a thumbs up. I had felt that Dr. Prezant had Al's best interests at heart, but I was still relieved to know that Al had heard that he was a good doctor.

I also have a good friend, Denise Evers, who is a nurse. She was wonderful. Her husband Richie is a retired firefighter who had worked with Al in Rescue 2, and Denise and Richie came to the hospital almost every day. Denise always put my mind at ease. She asked great questions, and she reassured me that the care that Al was getting was excellent. Denise and Richie's presence and support meant a great deal to me.

One morning towards the end of the first week, one of the doctors told me that Al's hemoglobin was so low that they were going to have to give him a transfusion. The hemoglobin reading was 8.5; if it went below 8, they would have to administer the transfusion. Fortunately, I had Dr. Prezant's cell phone number. Whenever there was a medical decision to be made, I would call him. He'd either talk to me directly or he would get back to me within five minutes. Naturally, I was reluctant for Al to have a transfusion. Dr. Prezant told me that there were no other options. The doctors and I spent that whole day checking the numbers. Al's hemoglobin level dropped to 8, but didn't fall any further. Each time there was a crisis, I would think this time was going to be it, but each time, Al would somehow fight his way through. The hemoglobin numbers crept up, so we never had to deal with the transfusion.

Another positive development that first week was that once taken off the respirator, Al never had to go back on it. They had started to wean him off it on Saturday. Originally, the doctors had decided to try him two hours off and two hours on, but very soon, they were saying, "He's doing so well, we'll give him another hour off the respirator." After Al had been breathing on his own for most of the morning and afternoon, the doctors decided to watch him for twenty-four hours to make sure he remained stable.

Now that he was breathing on his own, however, Al was more vulnerable to infection. People had been coming to see him, even though he wasn't always awake. At this point, the nurses told me, "You really shouldn't have too many people in here now. The more germs he's exposed to, the greater the risk." I passed the word along, and everyone was very understanding.

After a week at JCMC, the doctors felt that Al was stable enough to move to a hospital closer to home. Since Dr. Prezant was affiliated with Montefiore Hospital, in the Bronx, it made sense to move Al there.

I explained to the staff that we weren't leaving because we weren't satisfied with the care, only because it was easier for my family and me to travel back and forth. It was important to me to leave there, having them know that we appreciated all that they had done. I will always speak of the Jersey City Medical Center ICU staff with the highest regard. They saved Al's life.

Once the decision to move Al was made, the doctors at Jersey City wanted to make sure that all the things that needed to be in place, were. X-rays were taken, and a constant revolving door of specialists finalized their care. The doctors and nurses at JCMC sent much of his medical information with us, and other paperwork had been faxed over to Montefiore. Nobody missed a beat, in terms of Al's care.

Everything happened so quickly that the process was a little overwhelming. I had no time to prepare. Many of the doctors and nurses who had been caring for Al weren't on duty the day we left. I had thought I'd have the opportunity to say good-bye, and to thank them, because even though Al had been there only a relatively short time, I felt connected to many of the people there. They had been a great source of strength and support. Although I knew this was a positive step, a step forward, somehow, I longed for the security I was leaving behind.

Al was rolled out on a stretcher and placed in a critical-care ambulance. He was heavily sedated, but conscious, and really had no idea of what was happening. I got in the back of the ambulance, and two nurses joined us. Lorraine traveled with Mike Razzoli in his Jersey City Fire Department vehicle. Tom Murphy, a chief in the Jersey City Fire Department and who had been very helpful to me while Al had been in the hospital, joined in his fire-department car. A motorcade of police cars and fire department vehicles escorted us.

Our friends Richie and Denise, had gone thirty minutes ahead, to make sure everything was ready, and the Jersey City police coordinated our arrival, so that an NYPD police escort would meet us at the Holland Tunnel.

As we emerged from the tunnel, our motorcade made its way past Ground Zero. As a result of coordination efforts, many people had been alerted that a firefighter who had survived 9/11 was being transported by ambulance to a hospital in New York City. Unbeknown to us, many civilians and rescue workers had spontaneously made posters and makeshift patriotic signs out of pieces of wood and scraps of paper that read, "Thank you." "You are our hero." "We love you." I had never expected anything like this.

As our motorcade passed along avenues and streets, these wonderful, caring, thoughtful people lined the way, waving American flags. For blocks and blocks up the West Side Highway, people were waving and cheering and applauding.

Al was drifting in and out of wakefulness. I tried telling him everything that we were witnessing, but he wasn't aware enough to appreciate this outpouring of love. As we passed, I kept thinking how I wished he could see and experience this. He would have been so proud.

A little farther along, the crowd began to thin, and just as we thought everything had settled down, I caught sight of a lone, older man on the corner just to the right of us. He was standing at attention, and as the ambulance passed, he raised his hand and saluted Al, his eyes focused straight ahead, looking out onto the Hudson River. He never made eye contact, but stood like that, as the ambulance and the motorcade passed him. I was overwhelmed. He is etched in my memory forever.

CHAPTER TWENTY

MONTEFIORE HOSPITAL

As we passed through New York City, more NYPD vehicles joined us. By the time we reached Montefiore Hospital, we had six police cars ahead of us and close to that many behind us. Outside the hospital, several people were waiting to greet us. Al was taken inside quickly, and I went with him on the elevator to the Pulmonary ICU. I quickly realized how very comfortable I had grown to the original surroundings at JCMC. This new ICU was smaller, and because it was a Pulmonary ICU, it didn't have the individual nursing care that we'd had in the Surgical ICU in Jersey.

As they settled him in, we were surrounded by new doctors and an all new staff in a new situation. I tried to relax myself by thinking that since this was Dr. Prezant's hospital, everything would go smoothly; however, the reality was that I felt a little weary starting over again with new doctors and nurses. I'd already established such a good working relationship at JCMC. I hoped I'd be able to do it again.

Of course, things were different. First, Al was more alert. During his more lucid moments, he was making it very clear that he wanted to leave the hospital as soon as possible. Even though I knew this wasn't yet possible, I felt he deserved my best effort. One morning, I was standing near the nursing station and overheard one of the doctors say, "We're going to do the sleep apnea test on the firefighter."

When he finished, I went over to him and explained that I hadn't meant to be listening, but I wondered if it were my husband he'd been talking about. He said yes it was, and I asked what the sleep apnea test was and why he felt Al needed one.

"Well, Dr. Apple feels that your husband might have sleep apnea, and while he's here, we figured we'd do the test," he said.

I was a little surprised that they would plan something without consulting us first, and I mentioned this to him.

"Oh, don't worry," he replied.

Dr. Apple, the physician in charge wasn't available, so I waited and asked more questions to get an idea of what the procedure entailed. When Dr. Apple did arrive, he explained why they were planning to do the test. Apparently, Al had many of the physical characteristics typical of sleep apnea sufferers. "He could possibly die from sleep apnea," Dr. Apple said.

Until I heard that, I'd been certain that I'd try to convince him to wait on the test, but after hearing this news, I wasn't sure what to do. We talked in greater detail and finally decided that although Al might have the problem, perhaps under the circumstances, the test could wait. One of the main reasons that I didn't want Al to have the test was that he would have to stay in the ICU another day or two, and since he'd already gone through ICU psychosis, I didn't want him to have to endure that again. Each time I made a decision, I tried to put myself in his place.

There was another firefighter in the ICU from the World

Trade Center who had some lung problems, not as serious as Al's, but requiring surgery. He, too, experienced ICU psychosis. One night, after everyone had gone to sleep, he got up and entered the hallway, intent on leaving the hospital. Mike and I were asleep in the waiting room when we heard the screaming. Mike got up and managed to stop him. The firefighter was a big man, and I knew that I never could have restrained him.

Across the street from the hospital, there was a condominium complex, and the hospital was kind enough to give us keys to an apartment owned by them. We took turns going there for showers every day, but we preferred sleeping close to Al, at night.

It was good to get a shower. I didn't have to have anyone escort me, as I'd had in Jersey. In Jersey City, I had to carry my clothes into the shower room, and they would always somehow get wet. The condo had a regular bedroom, so I could lay my clothes on the bed, relax a little bit, and watch a little TV. There was a kitchenette, so we brought in some food. The apartment became a temporary refuge where I could take a break for an hour and renew my energy.

On the Tuesday after we'd moved Al to Montefiore, I decided to go home for a little while because I really wanted to see my children. Firefighter Tommy Wosca came by to drive me, and we left around 4 p.m. Al's sister Liz and his brother Rick stayed with him. By the time I got back, around 6:30 p.m., Liz was waiting downstairs for me. When she saw me, she greeted me with an anxious look and said, "There was a problem with Al."

"Oh my God."

"He's okay, but I'm concerned about his mental state," she said.

I immediately felt guilty that I'd left. "What happened?" I

asked her.

She explained that a doctor had come in to talk to Al, and Al had become very agitated.

When I got upstairs, he seemed calm. I was told that right after I'd left, a group of about ten firefighters came from the local firehouse in the Bronx. They all had become emotional and Al had, as well. This was the first large group of firefighters he had seen. It had been a charged moment. Later, Al wouldn't remember anything about the Montefiore ICU, but he did remember seeing the firefighters come in and salute him. They hugged him and told him they loved him, and Al said that they were "the best thing in the world."

After the firefighters left, a psychiatrist had come along. He started to talk to Al, and Al proceeded to tell him about his experiences in Oklahoma City. The doctor was concerned and asked Al if he could ask him some questions.

Al said the doctor raised the subject of death.

"I've seen enough death in my life," Al said.

"What do you mean?" the doctor asked.

"I was in Oklahoma City. There was death everywhere. We had to carry out the bodies. I think I've had enough. What I saw here on 9/11 ... the innocent civilians jumping. I think it's over for me. I've had enough."

When I spoke to the doctor, he told me that he felt that Al was overwhelmed. "People don't just tell strangers these kinds of things," he said.

I tried to assure him that for Al this wasn't unusual. "It doesn't take a lot for him to talk to people. He's a people person. You asked a direct question, and he answered you." I told him that I didn't consider anything that he'd described as out of the ordinary. "Maybe for some people, this would be an indication that something is wrong, but in this case, I don't think so," I said.

They weren't convinced, and recommended a psychiatric evaluation; then I started to question myself. The medical staff talked about post-traumatic stress syndrome, and I listened, but finally, I told them, "I know I'm not a doctor, but I think I know Al better than anybody here. Believe me, if I thought he was mentally unstable, I'd get him help. If he needs help when we go home, certainly, we'll seek it." Deep in my heart, I really wanted them to just leave us alone. I trusted that together we would find a way to figure it all out. They were pretty persuasive though, and in the end, I agreed to let someone talk to him. They promised to allow me to be there with him.

An interview time was arranged, and a psychiatrist came in at the designated hour. He had a very thick accent, which made it difficult for Al to understand what he was saying, and the doctor's attitude was very somber. He never smiled; he stood at the end of Al's bed and spoke to him very slowly. "How are you? How are you feeling?" he began.

Al mimicked the doctor by answering as best he could, holding his dressing over his stoma. "Good. How are you?"

I hadn't told him what was happening, and I felt sure that Al wasn't aware that this was a psychiatric evaluation.

The doctor asked a few more questions. No rapport was being established. I waited a few minutes, and then said to the doctor, "I think Al is a little tired. Maybe we can do this another time."

After the psychiatrist left, I contacted the original psychiatrist and said, "With all due respect, I'm sure that person you sent is a wonderful doctor, but I don't think we developed any rapport. Could you please send someone else? I also think Al needs to know what's going on. He's going to wonder why he's being asked all these questions."

The doctor allowed me to tell Al about the evaluation. He

agreed to it.

Another doctor came who turned out to be very nice. He sat next to the bed, close to Al. This doctor started by asking Al how he was, how his day was going. After a few minutes, he said, "I'm going to ask you a few questions, so just answer them to the best of your ability."

"All right," Al agreed.

"What's your name?" the doctor asked; then he asked other basic questions, like "What is your mother's maiden name?" After Al responded correctly to those questions, the doctor asked, "Can you recite the months of the year backwards?"

I saw Al's composure change. An intense look crossed his face. He clearly wanted to pass this test, so that he could get out of the hospital. He paused and seemed to seriously evaluate the doctor's question. He seemed to be searching, as if the question had some hidden meaning meant to trick him.

"Starting with December, 2001 or January, 2002?" he finally asked. He was trying to prove that he clearly understood that January of the coming year was 2002.

The doctor smiled. He told Al, "Starting with December."

I saw Al squint to concentrate. "December, 2001; November, 2001…"

The doctor smiled again. "Al, you don't have to say '2001' each time."

At that point, we all realized that Al's reasoning ability and state of mind were better than we'd thought, and I think we all felt more relaxed. We spoke for a few more minutes about our concerns and feelings, and the doctor gave us some good advice and wished us luck; then he shook Al's hand and wished him the best.

Al had arrived on Monday afternoon and was out of the Pulmonary ICU by Wednesday. He had to stay there because he'd had surgery to remove the tube inserted into his collapsed lung; they then took out the tube from the stoma in his throat. They didn't stitch the hole in the throat area closed. The doctors put a patch there, and said the skin would close over the hole naturally.

The ICU waiting room at Montefiore Hospital had two thick leather couches across from each other. Although they weren't very comfortable, we could at least stretch out. Those couches were like the Hilton, when compared to the vinyl upright chairs in Jersey City's ICU waiting room. I slept on one couch and Mike or Lorraine slept on the other, each of the nights we were there.

While we were at the two hospitals, Al and I were insulated from the outside world. I was totally focused on Al's recovery, while Al was focused on healing. Beyond the initial contacts and some visitors, we weren't yet dealing with the real sadness. When anyone came from the Fire Department, it was very difficult and very sad. It was easier for us to see people not connected to the Fire Department, because they provided a distraction or a moment away from the terrible sadness. I remember when Mary Beth Collins, a friend, brought Al a pair of shorts from St. John's University, because Al's such a big St. John's fan. We enjoyed a laugh; yet, while laughing, I realized how strange it actually felt to laugh. I didn't say anything, because I didn't want to ruin the moment, but I remember feeling very guilty.

CHAPTER TWENTY-ONE

9/11 – REALITY SETS IN

By Thursday, three positive steps had been taken: first, the doctors started weaning Al off some of the drugs, and as a result, he was beginning to think more clearly; second, he was moved into a private room, which gave us our first sense of privacy, since 9/11, and third, the hospital provided me with a cot, so that I could sleep next to Al in his room.

Sleep was very difficult for Al because he was in so much pain. I wasn't sleeping that well, either. Thoughts of other firefighters' families who'd lost loved ones were starting to creep into my thoughts, more regularly. The shock was wearing off, and reality was setting in. When we couldn't sleep, we used the time to talk.

I knew the time was coming to talk to Al about the magnitude of 9/11. I couldn't keep people at bay, any longer. He was in a regular room, and people wanted to visit him. A couple of close firefighter friends had come to talk to him, and they had begun to share some of the bad news. I wanted our conversation to be as natural as possible.

As the effects of the drugs began wearing off, Al's memory of 9/11 began to return, and what he recalled greatly disturbed his sleep. His first vivid nightmare in the hospital woke him. He began to cry saying, "Everybody's jumping. Everybody is jumping from the buildings, and I can't do anything." Later, he clearly would recall the people falling together and holding hands, floating down, then exploding. "I think I'm going crazy," he told me. "I keep dreaming of everybody jumping. I've got to talk to Father Judge."

"Father Judge?"

"I've got to talk to him," he repeated. "I've got to get this out."

The time had come. "Let's talk a little bit about that day," I said. "Just tell me what you remember."

"The entire South Tower collapsed," he said. "I remember seeing Pete Ganci and walking next to him, and then Ray came over." He recalled how Ray Downey and he "hooked up and talked about a third plane possibly coming in to attack us," and how they needed to help the trapped firefighters and civilians out of the partially collapsed Marriott and the collapsed South Tower. And he remembered Ray's saying, "Al, we just lost a lot of good people."

"Do you remember anything else?" I asked.

He concentrated for a moment and then said, "The North Tower collapsed?"

I nodded.

"Father Judge ...?" he asked in disbelief.

✲✲✲✲✲✲✲✲✲✲✲✲✲✲✲✲✲✲✲✲✲

AL'S COMMENTARY:

Eileen was trying to tenderly lead me in a direction that would help me understand without terribly shocking me. Now, I realized that the event was bigger than I had ever thought. I had to understand that we'd not only lost brothers in the first collapse, we'd lost even more in the second.

"Ray?" I asked very quietly, speaking his name almost reverently. I saw her eyes begin to well up with tears. She nodded.

"Pete Ganci also died?" I asked, and I saw in her eyes that she didn't want to deepen my pain with the truth. No words were necessary. I knew.

I asked about others, and finally, I just couldn't take it. Father Judge, Ray, Pete, and every other friend I named had died. "That's it! Stop. Don't tell me anymore."

Eileen came over to my bed and hugged me, and I started to cry uncontrollably.

"I wish I could tell you your friends were okay," she said softly.

After a few minutes, I lay back in bed and became completely quiet. I cried some more, and then I was spent. After that, I fell into a deep sleep.

This was one of the saddest days of my life. I was totally numbed, as I realized life was not to be the same. This frame of mind, combined with the medications, made me think that maybe I was dead too. How lucky could I have been to be the only one alive? No. I was really dead, and just didn't realize what was happening.

I refused to look at the list of those who had died. The list overwhelmed me. My memory was still faulty, so it was easy for me to miss the names of all those I knew, among the 343 names.

Brothers from nearby Bronx companies started coming in groups of six to twelve. These were very emotional visits, and very humbling. I felt that special connection again, with my brother firefighters and with America. It was also empowering to see their concern; their visits gave me the strength to try to get better.

Though the medicine and my disoriented brain still had me feeling outside myself, I knew that whether I was dead or alive, I wanted out of the hospital. I forced the issue of my leaving, and basically almost signed myself out. It may have been a mistake to leave so soon, but I was in a frenzy to get home. I wanted to be in that safe place, where I could try to get my thoughts together, which as yet, I hadn't been able to do. I wasn't thinking about all the mourning I had yet to experience; I just wanted to be home.

****

The doctors had to be convinced that Al was ready to leave, before they'd consider allowing him to go home. "I have a good friend who's a nurse," I assured them. "If I'm in trouble, I'll call her."

We'd been living in the moment, and I never realized how difficult it might be for me to dress his many wounds or nurse him on my own. My goal was simply to do whatever we could to get him home. Al's final 'test' was to show that he could walk unassisted, which was going to be difficult because he still had severe vertigo, caused by his head injury. The physical therapist, as well as the doctors, would have to decide whether or not he was well enough to leave.

Al was so determined that he forced himself to do things that he could not normally do. He rallied himself for that moment, and we finally got the doctors to agree that home would be a better place for him. Arrangements were made for him to leave the hospital on a Saturday morning. It seemed like a miracle that he was leaving just a few weeks after he'd been brought into the ICU with such severe injuries. Scott Hanson, the firefighter from the Marine Division assigned to help us, made all the arrangements. He met us at the hospital that morning.

When we walked out of the room, we were surprised to be greeted by the nurses and doctors, all lined up. They started applauding, as Al and I began walking down the hallway. It was a humbling experience for Al, because he didn't expect this attention. He could barely contain his emotions.

When we reached the street, Al was flabbergasted because there were fire trucks parked on the street, and fire-fighters were lined up along the sidewalk saluting him.

"I'm not leaving until I kiss each one," he said.

We had expected a private, quiet ride home. The applause, the saluting and the hugs gave Al a gigantic boost. All of a sudden, we saw a limousine.

"I don't want a limousine. I just want somebody to drive us back home in my car," he said. He was clearly embarrassed and uncomfortable.

Scott Hanson had arranged the limousine ride, and in order for Al to talk, he still had to hold the dressings against his stoma, so there was no way he could argue about the limousine. We both felt embarrassed, but we knew it was meant as a kind gesture. People were just trying to express their appreciation.

And so, still feeling self-conscious, we drove off, waving to everyone and feeling relieved to be heading home. Along the way, we saw American flags on almost every house. Until now, Al and I hadn't seen how Americans had come together and responded to the attack. Over the bridges and the overpasses of the highways, we saw draped flags and signs that read, "We love you, FDNY and NYPD." I could tell that this outpouring of love was good for Al. He would want to get strong. He would want to make these people proud.

As we neared Long Beach and our house, Al said to the

driver, "Could you please drive by the bank, so I can get some money to pay you."

"Get out of here. That's taken care of," he said, giving Al a big smile.

"Well, please let me give you a tip," Al said.

He gave Al an incredulous look, and hugged and kissed him.

Al, age 4, in Ecuador

Al with sister, Elizabeth, and Dad, Alfredo, in Ecuador

Al with mom, Aida, and Dad, Alfredo, at Promotion Ceremony in 1996

From left to right: Eileen, Lizzy (15), Al, Matthew (20), and Caitlin (18)

*From left to right: Norma (aunt), Liz (sister), Aida (Mom),
Alfredo (Dad), Al, Eileen, Ricky (brother),Gizelle (niece),
Adrian (sister), Victoria (sister-in-law)*

Al and Eileen at Promotion Ceremony to Captain in 1996

Al, Ray Downey and Richie Evers

Hurrican Hugo, Puerto Rico, 1989 – 1st deployment and
beginning of the FDNY NYTFI FEMA team.
Left to right: Ray Downey, Jim Rogers, a Puerto Rican officer
and Al.

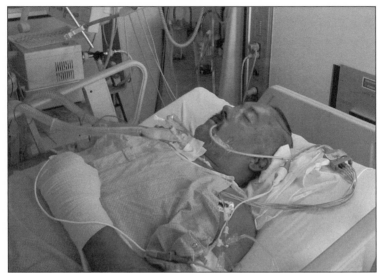

9/13/01 – Al in a drug induced coma at the Jersey City Medical Center Surgical ICU

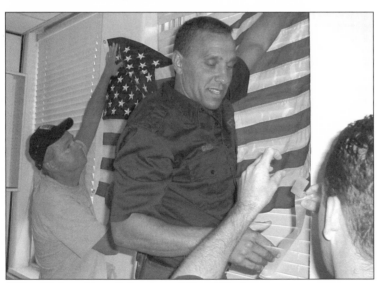

Mike Keilty, Don Galeoto and Tom Woska

Al reciting the "Pledge of Allegiance" at the Basilica of the National Shrine of the Immaculate Conception in Washington, D.C. on the 1st anniversary of the Sept. 11 attacks. Al was leading the Knights of Columbus contingent.

June 2002 – Surprise Reunion in Jersey City, Puccini's Restaurant, with staff of the Jersey City Medical Center Surgical ICU. Left to right: Mel (nurse), Mike Keilty, Lorraine Keilty, Owner Pasquale, Al, Sue (nurse), Eileen, Mike Razzoli, Darlene Razzoli

PART THREE
RECOVERY AND BEYOND

CHAPTER TWENTY-TWO

FIRST DAYS HOME

When the limousine pulled up to my house, I thought, what a wonderful sight. Only my children, Eileen and her parents were there. I didn't want anyone else to see me in what I considered my feeble state. With Eileen assisting me, we walked slowly up the path. The children had draped a huge American flag over the garage doors, and taped to the front door a beautiful hand-made sign on poster board with the flag and its stars in red, white and blue that read, "Welcome Home Dad," and underneath that, "We're so proud of our heroes." I began to cry as I made it through the front door. The reality of the moment was overwhelming. Hundreds of my brothers and thousands of civilians would never be able to experience this moment of coming home. It was too much to take in.

The first thing I did inside was sit down in my chair in our first floor den. The walk from the car to the front door and the emotional strain had exhausted me. I had no interest in talking to anyone. I just wanted to sit in my chair. I was quiet and somber. My children looked at me and looked afraid. They were probably worried that this was what I would be like for

159

the rest of my life. Eileen's parents were trying to be kind and make small talk, but my mind was far away. Having my chair was like having a security blanket. I needed that. Eileen placed the Oklahoma City blanket that was given to me years earlier, across my lap, and it felt good. That was all I wanted, the security of that blanket and chair. The ride home had been exhausting, and I had no energy left.

A few days later, the desire and the drive to get better came over me. I managed to walk back and forth from the chair to the wall of the den - a distance of about six feet - twice. That 'exercise' so exhausted me that I had to take a nap. I was a strapping 230 pound man with the balance of a toddler. Thank God I didn't have to do anything. Eileen took care of that. She took off from work for the next few months to stay with me. She was my angel, my nurse, my therapist, my support and my friend. She kept me alive.

While in the hospital, I'd told Eileen I felt as if I were in a different world, as if I were having an extended out-of-body experience. When I was lying in the hospital bed, I would hear voices, but nothing felt connected. I was so deeply drugged that my brain wasn't able to function normally; that's why I had wanted to be home. I wanted to get back down to earth and I hoped, get my life back. But coming home didn't solve all my problems. I still felt far away. I was in constant pain. My broken ribs weren't healing properly and my left lung was extremely sensitive; when I moved my head, the vertigo would cause my surroundings to whirl and spin at such a heightened speed that I would have to remain motionless for a long time to minimize the dizziness. After these episodes, I would collapse from exhaustion.

The chair in the den wasn't conducive to sleep, and while Eileen could have gone and bought another, my sister Elizabeth had called to see how I was doing, and said that she had a recliner that she wanted to give me. She and Joe brought it over to the house the next day, and it turned out to be a lifesaver. I could adjust it to the most comfortable angle to minimize the pain and vertigo. That recliner became my bed for the next eight months. I still often sleep in it.

Eileen and I started a twice-a-day routine of changing the dressings on my wounds. I was unsteady on my feet and needed someone to keep me balanced, so she would help me up the stairs. In that way, we could have privacy. A friend and nurse, Regina Milito, offered to help, and we thanked her, but it was this strong desire for privacy that determined our decision. After twenty one years of marriage, Eileen and I understood one another, so when my old take-charge self would try to take over and I would want to do too much, Eileen was there to patiently talk me out of it. She did everything and more that a home health care aide would have done. The changing of the dressings was only one of these tasks.

I would get all the bandages and tape from the bathroom and bring them over to the bed, and then I would sit while Eileen went about putting on the fresh gauze dressings. She would encourage me by telling me that I looked great compared to the way I'd looked in the Jersey City ICU, but I still had that nasty-looking head wound. We referred to a part of it as a 'divot,' the hole made when a golfer takes too much grass with a swing of the club. Something had hit part of my head, pushing in my skull and my skin. Pus sat in this divot as the skin and bone had gradually grown back. The doctors had told us that by applying moist gauze dressings twice a day, we would help with this skin growth.

The tracheotomy wound in my neck was still fresh, so we had to be careful of infection; I still had to put my hand over the dressing and wound whenever I wanted to talk, in order to minimize the escaping air, and promote the healing of the wound. The other major wound was on the left side of my chest, from the collapsed lung.

I think most of us assume that when a person returns home from a hospital stay, he's still the same person. I wasn't in any way mentally or physically the same. I believe I never will be. As long as I was in my chair, I seemed to be doing pretty well, but as soon as I would get up and start to navigate, I'd have to adopt an odd zombie-like walk, staring straight ahead, my eyes opened wide. I didn't want to look at anyone; I was literally trying to stare through everyone, in order to maintain my balance. The other mannerism I developed as a result of my excessive dizziness was to stand still with my head completely rigid. I could move it only in unison with the rest of my body, and then, very slowly, or I would fall over. I performed every movement very cautiously because of the vertigo. I had to be extremely careful because a fall could have resulted in more serious damage to my already broken ribs and barely protected brain.

Our home lies directly under the incoming flight path to J.F.K. Airport. When I would rest in my yard, the sound of any jet flying overhead set off an irrational fear that the plane was going to crash into my house. I would see bodies coming out of the sky. To someone else this sounds bizarre, but I learned it was a manifestation of my brain's trying to cope with all that had happened.

Eileen's father, who was accustomed to our usual joking relationship, found that I wasn't the same. "Did the head injury affect his thinking process?" he asked Eileen. Eileen's mother would look at me with tears welling up, and she would have to leave the room to cry. Many people found it disturbing to be around me. Some thought I looked and acted like a soldier experiencing shell shock; in a sense, that's what I was. I found noises – common household sounds like someone's dropping a phone receiver or a fork, or TV sounds – alarming. This symptom is common to people with head injuries. Even while sitting in my chair, I was afraid that something would fall off a bookshelf and hit me in the head again. I was absurdly protective of my head. Whenever anyone came close, I reacted by moving away, wanting to be by myself. Everyone, even my own children, naturally started asking, "Is he going to be like this forever?"

Eileen's parents stayed for the first two days after I came home; they could see that she was doing a good job in taking care of me. Eileen, who had been with me from day one in the hospital, was my lifeline to the real world. She kept reassuring me that I was gradually becoming more lucid, and that some of my thinking processes and old personality traits were returning. She had reason to feel more positive. I wasn't able to. My brain hadn't recovered, and I was still living in and out of a waking nightmare.

CHAPTER TWENTY-THREE

RECOVERY

In the past, under normal circumstances, I had always written the checks and paid the bills. Three months had passed, and we had reached the point of having to look at our finances. Eileen tried to get me started by just talking about the bookkeeping, but I couldn't perform any mental activity. When I would try to write a check, the mental effort would cause severe strain that in turn caused an excruciating headache, and I would have to stop and rest. I couldn't write a single check. I couldn't even read a few sentences of a newspaper. The skull fracture and head injury were still in the process of healing; all I could do was rest.

I recall conversing with people, but I really didn't take part in the conversations. I was in a fog and couldn't concentrate on the moment; my feet weren't planted on the ground and I felt cut off. Sometimes, I didn't even feel as if I were in the room. This lasted for a few months after I came home, and I wondered again if in fact, I'd actually died. During this same period, I was aware of several things: I knew I couldn't walk without someone's keeping me balanced; I knew I was sleeping or resting all the time, and I knew I had no energy. In the beginning, I expressed my frustration by getting angry.

Those last days in the hospital, Eileen had kept telling me how she saw me slowly becoming a little more mentally alert and upbeat; when I came home and saw my limitations, she felt I regressed mentally and lost some of my optimism. However, I did manage to maintain a determination to get better. The increasing awareness of 9/11 was beginning to affect me. I don't think I became depressed, but a great sadness came over me. I had anticipated that coming home would mean the cure to everything, but was struck by the realization that there was no fast cure for my body, my brain or the mental anguish that I was just beginning to experience.

In order to get myself released from the hospital, I had tried extremely hard to mask my physical problems with steady improvements, and with my upbeat attitude. As a result, I was probably released much earlier than I actually should have been. I knew I couldn't walk well. I was in severe pain and in a constant daze, and there was the never-ending vertigo; consequently, I had a great number of frustrations to get angry over, once I was home. It was killing me not to be able to function as a normal person would, and I would strike the arm of my recliner, in anger.

Once I was home, a fear that maybe I would never be able to overcome my limitations set in, and I would say to Eileen, "Honey, am I going to be a vegetable?"

She would try to calm me. "Al," she'd say, "you have to realize that just a few weeks ago you were in a coma. Now, you're able to do this. Focus on the growth that you've made, and don't put such high expectations on everything."

Somewhere along the way in those initial months at home, I came to realize that if I were ever to be an able person again, I'd have to go into higher gear. When I was able to reason more clearly, I decided that it was unacceptable to confine myself to living my life in a recliner. If I couldn't take care of myself, what would happen? Was I to be put in a home? Over the course of several months, I began to realize that I could not live this way; I had to take some form of action.

I devised a program of my own that consisted of daily sessions in which I would practice walking in our back yard. I would begin by leaning against a tree; then I'd start out on my own wobbly legs for the next tree. When I reached it, I'd slap the branch with its overhanging leaves, encouraging myself that I had made it to that point. I would then head for the next tree across the yard, and when I reached that one, I'd slap a branch of it.

I must have been an odd sight, practicing my walking, going from tree to tree, slapping each one; little did I know that my children were keeping an eye on me from the kitchen window, amused.

Eventually, I was ready to venture beyond the house. Eileen told me that she was afraid I'd try to go too far. "You might push yourself and walk to a point that you can't walk back from." She made sure that there was always someone to walk with me, to and from the stop sign, about a block away, and whenever she heard the front door, and saw me going out, she'd automatically call out to Lizzy, "Daddy just went out. Go walk with him and make sure he's okay." I would get annoyed at having someone with me at all times, but I guess it was better to be cautious. Once I'd get back inside from those very brief walks, I would sit in my recliner and go to sleep for two hours; that's how much they tired me out.

As I became stronger, Eileen and I started to walk from home to the boardwalk – a distance of about a mile – and then along the boardwalk, once a day. Sometimes, we'd sit on a bench and reflect on the beauty and solace of the waves and the beach. We tried to walk every day, and were lucky to have a warm winter. That weather - so mild for the New York City area - allowed us to experiment with going outside more often. The walks were invigorating, a healthy refuge from sitting in my recliner all day.

Sometimes though, sleep also acted as a shelter. Sleep provided a way to escape reality for a while and recharge the little energy that I had. Eileen and I were taking in an overwhelming amount of information about death as we learned of the number of firefighters, other emergency rescuers, and all the civilians who had perished, a number reaching into the thousands. It was hard putting all that sadness into our heads at one time. Sleep gave us moments of peace. While I slept in my recliner in the den, Eileen slept right across from me on our large sofa. We spent a lot of time talking, which helped me to reflect and put the pieces together of what had happened to the many firefighters I had known, and to try to begin to understand the reason that I had survived. I was beginning to experience "survivor's guilt."

Initially, after coming home from the hospital, I didn't feel the need to talk to a therapist. In the fire department, we like to think of ourselves as macho, as not needing a professional's help. A good friend of mine encouraged me to go to the therapist he was seeing, and I did. Dr. Jennifer Roberts, who is connected to Cornell Medical Center, works with firefighters in the Burn Center. I call her a "firefighter's angel."

The primary issue that I had to work through was this "survivor's guilt." I had come out of the rubble alive, but I was older than many of my brothers who had died, and my guilty thinking would tell me that I should have died so that a younger firefighter could enjoy helping his children grow up. I would think about that every day.

Amid all the frustrations and all the progress, something

else became apparent. We had more friends than we'd ever realized. In those early days, we never had to cook a meal for ourselves, because some of our neighbors and close friends had pre-arranged to bring meals to us. It was humbling to know that people in the neighborhood – some of whom we'd never met – wanted to show their support and affection by cooking for us and bringing us a meal.

Someone would knock on the door and Eileen or the children would answer. I'd be lying back in the recliner unable to move very quickly. People would look real fast to the right to see me in the den, but were afraid to stop and talk. Our good friends Tara and Billy Carlo would bring a plate of meatballs into the kitchen and then leave right away, afraid to initiate a conversation with me. I'd begin thinking that I must look like a zombie, but then I'd quickly think how nice of them to do what they were doing.

Sometimes, the doorbell would ring and there'd be a delivery of flowers or a plant. People would drop by to drop off a card. I really didn't want people to see me in the state I was in; however, I realized that every time the doorbell rang, I tried to act healthier, and in reality, I felt stronger!

There's something to be said about other people's kindness and the powerful, healing it produces. I never realized the power of a hug, a card or a letter, but I quickly learned to feed off these acts of kindness. These people who were showing me their love made me come to believe that I had to get better for them. Clearly, I had to get better for myself, but they also wanted me to get better, and I somehow reasoned that if I didn't, I'd be letting them down. Eileen told me that "the common thread" that has held true throughout my whole life, "and the reason that you've had success is that whatever the situation might be, you have this unique ability to find some type of catalyst, and you use that as your reason to improve."

She went on to say that whenever I experienced something negative, I was always able to find some way to dig out something that motivated me to become better. "The kindness of those people sending things over is only part of your recovery. Your real recovery comes from your attitude."

I was amazed and delighted when a neighbor who lived a couple of blocks away, whom I had never known, wrote me a two page letter about what I meant to her. In a sense, that letter was for the many rescuers who had died while assisting during the attacks, and it was for those who were continuing to assist now in the recovery efforts. These good-natured neighbors just wanted to say thank you and needed someone to express it to. There were so many people doing something special to encourage me; I just can't say enough about how humbled I felt or how those acts of kindness had such healing power. I got closer to so many neighbors and visitors.

Kathleen Harms, a friend and the mother of my daughter Lizzy's friend Kelly, came by and brought me an Irish blanket. I alternated this blanket with the Oklahoma City blanket, to cover myself with in the recliner.

Friends would call to say that they were treating us at a local Italian restaurant and wanted to know what night would be good for us to receive the delivery, and people were so thoughtful about what they brought. They made an extra effort to find out what my favorite foods and favorite meals were.

Greg Sinto, a neighbor, knew that I was allergic to clams, but that I love fish, so he baked a beautiful loaf of bread and made a fish chowder, and brought it over for lunch. "Why don't you sit down and join us?" Eileen asked him. He was nervous when he started out, but by the end of his visit, we had our bread and chowder and were chatting.

Another friend knew that I love the game of basketball

and somehow contacted some basketball personalities. Coach "K" at Duke University, Mike Krzyzewski, now a friend, wrote a book called *Leading With the Heart,* and mailed me a copy. When I opened the package and saw the title, it meant something special to me because I believe I've always tried to lead with my heart, and so have many of my brothers. Coach "K" wrote a beautiful message inside, and after reading his note, I cried and continued to get healthier.

I cried so much during this part of my recovery that I thought I was never going to stop. My emotions ran fever high, and the sadness and enormity of what had transpired were sometimes too much for me to handle, but every time I cried, I felt myself getting stronger and healthier. I felt appreciated and cared for, and I wish to thank all the people who showed their affection, for inspiring me.

Many wrote cards and letters, and these made me feel good because it became clear that my brothers and the civilians were remembered as well, that their deaths hadn't been in vain. At the same time, the memories tore at my heart. Most of the letters were saying, "You firefighters have made us feel so proud to be Americans. I'm so sorry for your loss."

Helen Rizzuto, one of our neighbors and an English teacher at a gifted school in Queens, had her classes 'adopt' me after learning that I had grown up in Queens. Every week, I received letters that were very thoughtful and sophisticated, and I corresponded with the students through Helen. Eventually, I went there to talk to them, to personally thank them for their efforts, and to tell them what it meant to do what they had done.

These cards, letters and acts of kindness changed my life. School children from South Carolina, Illinois, Florida and around the country were sending me mail. My longtime friend John Kaslyn's wife Pat, a school teacher in Illinois, had her class send me cards every week. The mail carrier would deliver so many cards and letters each day that I needed a carton in which to store them. Since I couldn't get out of my chair very much, it was wonderful to be able to sit there and read. I read each one of those cards and letters.

Erica Petrilli, from Great Falls, Montana, a competitor in the Special Olympics held in Montana, won a gold medal in the 25m walk. Incredibly enough, in the aftermath of 9/11, Erica wrote me a beautiful letter and sent me her medal, saying, "You're my hero. I'm thinking about you." What can I possibly say? I was extremely humbled by her act and expression of love. I wrote her back saying how overwhelmed I was by her generosity, and her father Don wrote to tell me how much she appreciated my letter. "Erica also loves to compete in basketball; she's small, but that doesn't stop her from giving her best," he wrote. Here is a girl who has some "limitations," I thought, yet she's out competing, and giving her best. Here I was, a 230 pound man. Could I really just sit around and feel sorry for myself? I had to give my best, also, and maybe, just maybe, I would become as big a person and meet the standards Erica had so lovingly shown me. America is filled with wonderful people.

As I'd begun to learn earlier, hugs were an important part of my recovery. A friend would come in and we would hug, and I would feel stronger and more committed to the idea of improving. I had first learned about the art of hugging when I'd gone with the NYTF 1 FEMA team to help out at the Oklahoma City bombing. Ray Downey and I used to call it an "Oklahoma hug." As the rescuers came off the pile from a day of digging, the people would stand there and applaud. "Do you mind if I have a hug?" someone would ask me (something that as New Yorkers, we don't get a request for, often). "A hug? Okay," I would say, and we would hug, and then the person would start crying. I soon realized that it was a good feeling that empowered me to continue. I felt better, and the civilians felt as if they had contributed, and they had. The people of Oklahoma City taught me the power in a hug. I hug more, now.

Very often, our visitors would get emotional. I found I spent a lot of time, saying "Don't worry. We're good," and "I'll be fine." I had made a shrine on my bookcase for my friends and the firefighters who were lost. There were the many Mass cards with their pictures from the memorials and funerals that I was able to attend, and the many that I was not able to. As soon as our visitors saw the shrine, they became overwhelmed. It was such an emotional time for everyone. I guess I represented their only connection with Ground Zero, and all the emotions they felt about the tragedy came pouring out in our den, as we shared our memories and grief.

One friend with whom I'd worked in the F.D.N.Y. was Jay Leach. Jay's son, Brian was a high school Junior who played basketball, and Jay and I used to go and watch him. Brian decided he wanted to visit me, and brought me a sausage and pepper hero. I was so appreciative that this young man took the time out of his life to visit me. Months later, when I was finally able to write a few sentences to thank people, I sent Brian a thank-you note. One day, Brian's mother Nancy, saw Eileen and said, "Oh my gosh. When Brian got that letter from Al, he brought it upstairs to his room, where he hangs photos of the professional athletes he admires. I have to tell you, Al's letter went above everyone else."

George Kreusher, a good man and retired brother firefighter from Rescue 1, came by. We'd studied for the Lieutenant's test together. George has two boys, both firefighters, who carry on the tradition in his family. He brought me a book on the Marines of Iwo Jima during World War II called *The Flag of Our Fathers.* George seemed to be saying, "Come on, Al. You know what you're capable of. I know you. You know yourself. You're getting through this." He was very upbeat and encouraging.

Dan Rather, the CBS News anchor; the *Today* morning show, and many others sent me a plant or flowers or cards. Of course, they wanted an interview, and I was in no condition. I couldn't and wouldn't grant any interviews, while the digging at Ground Zero continued for my brothers and the innocent civilians.

One particular individual from the Fire Department and some friends became adamant with Eileen and barraged her with reasons as to why she needed to do the interviews. They argued, "You should do something. It doesn't have to be anything big." Eileen felt the whole matter was getting out of control. Prime time newscasters wanted to do a special segment regarding my distressed radio transmissions from when I was trapped inside the rubble of Ground Zero. For a while, she'd been able to push off the media with excuses about my health and time. But now, even some close friends were asking that I agree to be interviewed; they felt that my surviving the collapses was one of the only positive outcomes of the disaster, and that it would be nice for the public to hear something positive. Eileen told everyone, "We don't think we should be on TV, while other people's husbands or family members have died, and all these tragic events have occurred. Those are the people that we care about." She made it clear that she felt that their stories were the important ones.

In addition to the visits, and the mail, I received several letters and phone calls from fire departments across the country. Eileen took all the calls because I couldn't hold a telephone conversation. Many of the fire departments called because they knew me and they knew some of those we'd lost, from the National New York City Emergency Response Teams. "I'll let Al know that you called," Eileen would tell them. "He really appreciates it. He's just not up to a lot of conversation."

Some of the out-of-town firefighters asked to stop by when they were in New York, so I knew I would be getting more visitors in the months ahead. Each visitor had a message for me: "We're counting on you to get better." I couldn't let any of them down.

The day came when Eileen and I had to discuss what she should do about her job. She had stayed out of work since 9/11, to help me. The school where she worked –Lindell School –had a substitute teacher filling her position. Eileen had never anticipated having to be out so long, and finally her principal, Karen, had to tell her that if she wasn't planning on coming back within the next two weeks, they'd have to get another substitute.

Eileen and I talked about the situation. The children in the classroom had gotten used to the sub and Eileen didn't want to put them through having to adjust to another teacher, only to then have Eileen return, which would make for yet another adjustment. We made the decision that she should return to school after Thanksgiving. I felt that I could be on my own, and the doctor agreed that I would be fine for a few hours; besides, Eileen worked only about five minutes away. If I had an emergency, she could get back to the house quickly. She planned on leaving around 8 a.m. and coming back at 11:30 for lunch; then she'd go back to school and be home by 3:15 p.m. Her coming home for lunch assured us that I wouldn't be left alone for more than a few hours at a time. Karen was very accommodating and was great about giving Eileen that flexibility.

The time alone forced me to become more independent.

As for the telephone calls, I just let people leave messages on the answering machine. Matt had decided to attend a local college for the year, in order to be available, and he helped out also.

I napped a lot, so I couldn't get into too much trouble. My constant napping made me self-conscious, though, because I hated for my children to see me sleeping so much. If I heard the front door, I'd sit up and try to look alert. It was all about being a good role model. I wanted to look as if I were staying awake, while getting through the hardest part of my recovery.

I also kept busy by going to physical therapy. There was vestibular therapy, hand therapy, back therapy and so on. I'd decided to perform my own routine at the Long Beach Recreation Center with the help of a therapist friend. Eventually, I was to extend my physical therapy to five days a week, as I was determined to get better faster. Brian O'Flaherty also went to physical therapy for rehab on his shoulder. He would pick me up at home, and he would drive and take me out for short walks on the boardwalk. It must have been funny watching the two of us, each with his own disabilities and injuries, tagging alongside each other on the beach.

On his days off, my brother Ricky took the time either to help me learn to use the computer or to bring our parents to visit, as they didn't drive. Thanks to him, I was able to keep busy with my computer and my newly acquired knowledge.

Another part of recovery included avoiding anything on TV about 9/11. Eileen would tell people "Al is showing he's smart enough to protect himself, mentally. He knows what he can and cannot handle." She was right. I just couldn't cope with the terrible tragedy of that day. I could only accept that it had happened.

We had to make several adjustments in our lifestyle. In the

past, we'd done things like getting dressed and getting off to an event, rapidly. Now, I could do nothing fast. We had to adjust to the fact that going somewhere required a lot of pre-planning. And faced with yet another frustration, I was not the friendliest of persons. Regardless of the cause of my anger – whether it was my inability to attend to my own head wounds or tie my own shoes - Eileen had the patience of an angel and the wisdom to know that my reactions stemmed from the vulnerable position I found myself in.

Eileen and I tried going to a couple of wakes and funerals each week, but for each one we were able to attend, we missed so many more. I just didn't have the energy to go out, so we concentrated on going to the funerals and memorials of those with whom I had been very close.

I think my first day to travel out of the house was to attend Timmy Higgins' memorial. Timmy was a close friend, brother firefighter and one of the toughest men I had known. We had worked together in Rescue 2 in Brooklyn and had fought many fires together. I was determined to pay my friend the respect he so justly deserved. Eileen considered my degree of determination a good barometer. Some time later, she told me that the firefighters there had noticed that I had taken on that zombie demeanor again; they said nothing to me, but their faces showed their concern.

Another time, Eileen and I attended a memorial for another very close firefighter friend of mine, Jack Fanning. Jack and I had shared adjoining offices at the Brooklyn Navy Yard. He was in charge of the Haz-Mat Operations, and we had also worked together in the aftermath of the Oklahoma City bombing. The day of Jack's service, the rain was pouring down. I'm sure Eileen didn't think it was a good idea that I go out, but she didn't want to suggest that we not go. Before we got to the church, the police had closed off the block.

"Why don't I just drive up and tell them who we are, and that it's a little hard for you to walk. They could let us through," Eileen suggested.

I'd have nothing to do with that. I preferred shying away from any special attention. I felt it only proper that we park in the assigned location, and that I walk to Jack's service. We parked two blocks from the church. Eileen and I got out and faced a stiff blowing wind that tore at the umbrella. By the time we got to the church, I was exhausted and a little disoriented. Eileen had noticed that whenever we went out, I would become much more disoriented than when I was at home.

Outside the church, people right away came up to say hello and hug. The present Chief of the Department, Chief Frank Cruthers, came over and said, "Al, why don't you go inside? We'll get you a seat inside."

"No, I want to salute Jack and pay him my respects," I said.

Eventually, I saw the fire truck arrive without a casket, and I saw a firefighter carrying a chief's white helmet. Sometimes, the services still had caskets, even if the body hadn't yet been recovered. After waiting a while, I began to understand. "Jack's not coming. Right?" I said to Eileen.

"No, I think it's a memorial. I don't think Jack was found, Al," she said in a low voice.

I so much wanted to properly salute my friend. It was all so unfair. My brain went into its frustration mode; I looked over at Eileen and said, "I have to go. I can't stay."

The people there were great. Those around us understood. We walked slowly away from where we had been standing outside the church. I couldn't stay for the service for Jack, and I was angry and profoundly sad, as this was becoming the norm.

CHAPTER TWENTY-FOUR

THE NURSES

As I was gradually getting healthier, the day arrived that I wanted to return and visit the nurses and doctors at the Jersey City Medical Center, and eventually, those at Montefiore Hospital, to say thank you. I had no recollection of who these people were or what they looked like, even; I only knew that they had saved my life. In anticipation, I had a beautiful plaque made up to present to the Surgical ICU staff.

Eileen has said that the day I returned was one of those moments when I was at my best; I went there believing that I was healthy enough to deliver my message of thanks. My brother Rick had taken digital pictures when I was in the ICU, so I had been able to see myself as a patient, and see the actual bed in the ICU where I was treated. When I entered the ward, I immediately looked in the corner to see where my bed was, and it was exactly as it had been in the photograph. I thought, that's where I almost died, and a sensation of extreme sadness and at the same time, gratitude, for what these doctors and nurses had done, overwhelmed me.

One of the nurses of whom Eileen was particularly fond –

Sue – was supposed to have come, but she had broken her foot and was out of work at the time; however, almost all of the doctors and nurses who'd treated me were there. The hospital had notified the staff and the media of my intentions. Cameras were recording everything. Everyone who had been involved in my treatment was standing at the nurses' station in the center of the room.

I began reading what I had prepared: "The North Tower collapsed, and I lay trapped. I believe there were angels all around us that day. These angels quietly guided rescuers to locate me; they assisted in recovering me from the rubble. These angels then arranged for me to be brought by fireboat to the Jersey shorefront ... I was having extreme difficulty breathing. Then suddenly, I remember hearing divine, soft voices, and there were all these angels running around my bed, caring for me, cleaning me, suctioning me so that I could breathe easier. These angels were rubbing me, saying, 'I'm here for you, Al. I'm here for you.' I have never seen live angels, and yet, today, at this wonderful moment, these angels are standing before me and I can finally see their faces."

I was trying to maintain my composure because firefighters are supposed to stay in control. I saw the various TV news cameras filming, and I didn't want to be a spectacle; however, I was so overcome that my emotions overtook me, and a steady stream of tears began to roll down my face. I turned to my right to get some support from Dr. Ford, who had operated on me and had been responsible for my care, but he was also in tears, and we hugged. Needless to say, everyone in the room was crying. I believe that all the feelings that our country was feeling about 9/11 over the losses we had suffered overcame us, and we just let them out. All of us were caught by how emotional the moment was. When I was finally able to finish, I said, "Nine-eleven happens to you every day. I'm alive today because of you."

Another special nurse, the only male nurse, was Mel. "Mel did everything for you," my friend Mike would tell me, when I was at home recovering. Most of the nurses, over the course of time, had warmed up to Eileen and to my visitors, but Mel was more reserved. He had a strictly professional attitude. Eileen described him as a phenomenal nurse who took excellent care of his patients. The day that we returned, Eileen watched Mel. He smiled that day.

A few months later, I paid the Jersey City Fire Department a visit. They had helped Eileen and my friends during my stay at JCMC in so many ways. I presented them with a plaque also. To my surprise, Coach Bob Hurley of St. Anthony's High School in Jersey City, who has since become a good friend, was there to present me with a basketball signed by himself and by his sons Bob, Jr. and Danny, who had played college basketball. Bobby had gone on to the pros. It was a lovely gesture from a person I admire.

After this event, I wanted to treat the Jersey City firefighter Mike Razzoli, his wife and our friends Mike and Lorraine to lunch. I had bought a crystal American flag paperweight for each of them, and engraved on the base of each was "9/11/01 – Thank you from Captain Fuentes," to present to them for all the help they had provided our family, during our time of need. I said, "Let's go to Puccini's," the Italian restaurant that had sent over the food to the hospital.

On an earlier day, I had stopped by that restaurant to thank the owner for his generosity, and to have my picture taken with him. When we took the picture, I was in uniform. I put my arm around him and said, "I can't say enough for what you did." "You know, Al, when I came here to the United States, I had nothing. Look at what I have now. At least, I can give back," he said.

I'd had this picture framed to present to him. We walked into that Italian restaurant with no idea of what was about to happen. I think it was Eileen who tapped me on the shoulder and said, "Do you see who's over there at that table?"

"Who?" I said.

"Look," she said.

It was early afternoon; the table she was talking about was filled with women and one man.

"They're all the nurses from the JCMC ICU who took care of you," she said. And then, I heard her say, "Oh my gosh, there's Sue!"

"It's Sue," Mike exclaimed, at almost the same time.

Eileen and Mike had always talked to me about Sue. They loved her. Whenever Eileen had had a question, the other nurses would say, "Talk to Sue." She had a spiritual perspective on everything, and was very calming. Eileen considered her very knowledgeable about nursing. I'd always said that we'd find out when Sue was working, and we'd go back and visit. I'd wanted to meet her.

When Sue had seen us walk in, she started to cry. She got up and started toward me, and I began walking toward her. We met somewhere halfway and hugged. I had finally met her.

"I have to tell you a couple of stories about your struggle in the ICU," she said, rubbing my hand. "I think I could try to explain why you survived; I believe I know the type of person you are. When you first were brought into the Emergency Room, I was with you every minute. I kept watching you. There was something about you. I don't know what it was. Your condition was extremely critical; your vital signs were failing. You were dying. Then, all of a sudden, you would do something, and you'd start moving. And your vital signs would begin to improve. I watched this cycle repeat itself many times. You're a fighter. There was no way that you wanted to go."

I became emotional and said, "The Man upstairs didn't want me yet, and I didn't want to go yet."

"I don't know if we can ever explain what happens," Sue said. "I've seen plenty of people. Your stats were declining. You must have fought numerous times. I didn't think you were going to make it, but then you would always do something to fight back."

Eileen remembered that with her quiet wisdom, Sue had told me as I left the JCMC ICU for Montefiore Hospital, "Now, you're going to have to fight further. This is going to be the hard road, but you have what it takes." That's the kind of person she is, a guide who leads you to the next level.

After all of us recognized each other, we got up and started hugging and taking pictures. The restaurant owner came out, and we told him what had happened. It seemed that one of the nurses was celebrating a birthday. They explained that they never usually went to that restaurant, but had chosen it that day. It was an honor to be in their presence, to be able to thank them again for what they had done for my family and me, for what they do every day, and to be able to treat them to a meal.

A few weeks later, I was able to visit Montefiore Hospital's Pulmonary ICU and thank them also for the extraordinary nursing care with which they'd showered me. They also had media coverage, and this time, I was a little more in control and delivered my message without any tears.

One of the nurses took me aside and quietly asked me if I remembered a conversation that I'd had with her. As I had been heavily drugged at that time, I said that unfortunately, I couldn't remember. She proceeded to tell me that when I was transferred from Jersey City Medical Center, she was trying, at one point, to further clean my fingers and my nails. She was trying to get the dirt from underneath. She said I suddenly asked her, "What are you doing?" and she replied that she was cleaning my fingertips.

"Do you remember what you said to me?" she asked. I didn't. "You said, 'You will never get my fingers clean.' They were full of burnt tar and debris, and I said, 'Of course, I will. Why wouldn't I be able to get it off?' and you answered, 'No. I was using my fingers to try and dig my way out. I don't think that tar will ever come off.'"

That story had stayed in her mind, and she started crying retelling it.

These are the types of individuals these ICU nurses from these hospitals are; I'm sure that nurses throughout this great land are similar, astonishing, knowledgeable professionals who love what they do, and who do it well. They are from all walks of life, all nationalities, and have, as the Fire Department does, a commitment to life. I will be indebted forever to these great nurses.

CHAPTER TWENTY-FIVE

CAITLIN FUENTES, AGE 18
9/10/02

In the first two weeks of my freshman year at Boston College, I felt well adjusted and happy in my new environment. I was growing to love the city of Boston, my new college and the new friends I made. However, on the eve of 9/11, the one-year anniversary of the attacks, memories of the tragedy began to consume my thoughts. I felt a strong need to be with my family, especially my brother and sister. We had been through so much together. It just felt wrong not to be in New York.

My roommate was from Florida, so she didn't know anyone who had been involved in 9/11. No one around me had experienced 9/11 the way I had. I called my boyfriend, Mark, who was attending Loyola College in Maryland. As soon as I heard his voice, I began to cry. I started to tell him stories beyond what my dad had gone through. I told him about Ray Downey and Lee Ielpi's son and many stories of the firefighters who had been tragically killed. He listened and comforted me. After we talked, he gave me the best advice. "You need to find someone there to talk to."

I walked out into the hallway, where I met Megan, Tabatha and Amy who had become my new friends. They saw my eyes were red from crying. I told them why I was upset, and I began crying again.

"Let's go down and talk to the peer minister in our dorm. We'll go down with you and we'll talk to him," my three friends encouraged. We went down, but he wasn't there, so we left a note under his door.

About fifteen minutes later, he came to my room where he talked with the four of us. I was telling them stories of what we had been through on 9/11 with my dad. I had known these people for only two weeks, but I wanted to tell them as much as I could.

That night, the peer minister was holding a remembrance ceremony for the 9/11 victims at Trinity Chapel. Everyone at the mass that night had a lit candle. With the lights turned off, we said a couple of prayers. Then the minister invited people to share what they wanted, about 9/11. It was quiet for a minute. Finally, a student stood up. He said that he lived in New Jersey and had seen the tragedy at the Twin Towers. Others stood up to tell their stories. Some people had relatives who had been involved, but no one knew anyone who had died.

"Come on. You can do it. Just stand up," Tabatha kept whispering to me.

Finally, I had the courage to stand up, and I said, "My father was a firefighter at the Towers. He was seriously hurt. I just want to ask you guys to remember him and all my dad's friends, because I know he's having a hard time right now. I don't think a lot of us would have done the same thing that they did."

September 11th was a lot better. I had gotten all my crying

out the night before. I wore my F.D.N.Y. Rescue 2 T-shirt all day to honor my dad's friends and all the fallen firefighters. What surprised me was that so many students were coming up to me and saying, "That memorial was so great. I'm so glad you stood up. Tell your dad we're praying for him. I'm so glad I went. I didn't realize how much it affected certain people. I didn't know anyone who had been hurt."

I had learned many things over those two days. I realized how close my brother and sister and I had become, after the attacks. I wanted to be with them and talk to them so much that day. We all had learned so much together about what it means to be brave and go the extra mile, and we had learned a lot about each other and how family is so important.

CHAPTER TWENTY-SIX

RETIREMENT

I knew that my career was coming to an end, because my injuries were so many and so severe. Any one of them would have kept me from remaining a full duty firefighter, but I was good at pushing that thought to the back of my mind. The New York City Fire Department had been my life. In many ways it had defined me: the kind of person I am, the beliefs I hold true. I lived, breathed and slept firefighting. How do you retire from that type of profession?

While I was recovering, most of my time was occupied with doctors, medical procedures, physical therapy and other medical issues. My focus was on getting myself back to as normal as possible. On Sundays, I would regularly see Dr. David Prezant at the F.D.N.Y. Bureau of Health Services at 9 Metro Tech, in Brooklyn. The doctors would not let me drive, so Eileen drove me to my early appointments, and then the Marine Division would assist in getting me to my other various doctors.

During the course of one of these examinations, Dr. Prezant said, "Al, I hope you realize that eventually there is going to be an end, here." He was gently trying to make me aware that retirement was a certainty, that there would be no options. He knew how intense a person I am; he knew the companies that I had worked at and that I had lived for the job. And now, I had almost died for the job. Regardless of how improved my condition might become, I was not going to be allowed back; the realization hit hard. Even before he brought up the issue of retirement, I had begun thinking of myself as a burden; I felt I was a burden to my wife and that I was becoming one to my children, also.

For the time being, I continued to focus on my therapy. The physical therapy helped tremendously with the injuries to ribs, hands, lungs and back; it also alleviated my vertigo. Four to five days a week, I would perform a workout from 10:30 in the morning to half-past noon, at the Long Beach Recreation Center. There I could use the weights room, where I could press light weights to strengthen my back and my hands; I also walked on the treadmill and used the exercise bikes. The swimming helped develop my lung capacity, and with the side to side movement of my head, my vertigo eased. I would periodically have to stop and 'recalibrate' myself before continuing, but I never missed these sessions.

I wound down the many doctors' visits, although some issues remained: my severely damaged lungs would need constant evaluation; the thoracic-rib situation, the vertigo, the loss of movement in some of my fingers and the back problems were all ongoing. Of the nine initial broken ribs, five had healed, but four would not and created severe pain by striking major nerves. I conferred with a few surgeons, and they said that the procedures that they would have to perform to properly repair the ribs would create more pain in the future. And so, I began looking into pain management. I conferred with physicians at St. Luke's-Roosevelt Hospital in Manhattan, about the possibility of killing the nerves that the ribs were striking. The doctors warned that the needle they would use to identify and then kill the nerves, sometimes caused the lung to collapse. In the end, I told them no, I had been down that route before. All I could do was deal with the pain management on my own.

"Al, whenever you're ready, we can begin the retirement process," Dr. Prezant said. He had been more than accommodating, in not pushing me too soon. I had finally arrived at the point at which I needed to set things in motion, because I felt as if I were in limbo. I realized that retirement was the first step I would need to take, in order to move towards beginning a new life and career. "It's time for me to get out," I told him, "and I want you to board me." 'Boarding' refers to the three step process of retirement.

February 1st, 2003 was suddenly around the corner, and I found myself telling Eileen, "Thirty days, and I'm going to be a civilian." I dreaded the day, but Eileen, who had been through so much already, and was now also dealing with my issues with retirement, continued to encourage me.

On January 31st, 2003, I had to hand in some of my equipment, bunker gear and whatever Department property I had left. I'd lost most of my equipment when it was cut off me on 9/11, and had never recovered it at the hospital. I'd lost my helmet and radio also, so I filled out a Lost Property Report.

On February 1st, 2003, I retired with a normal pension at half-pay. My disability papers were filed with the retirement papers. Sometime in the future, I'll appear before the third and final board, and they'll make a determination as to whether or not I should be retired on disability.

I reported to the F.D.N.Y. Headquarters at 9 Metro Tech in Brooklyn New York, and as I walked into the lobby, I did what I had always done in the past. I walked over to the large memorial plaque on the lobby wall that contains the names of firefighters who have died in the line of duty. I couldn't help but notice all the new names that had been added to the wall of honor, as a result of the sacrifices made on 9/11/01 in the attacks on the World Trade Center. I looked at the names of so many of my friends: Pete Ganci, Ray Downey, Dennis Mojica, Jack Fanning, Timmy Higgins, Terry Hatton. The list went on and on. I said a prayer, but the reality of the tragedy continued to elude me. I still couldn't believe it had happened. I saluted and slowly left.

Firefighting is basically a young man's job. When you reach your fifties, it gets harder and harder to climb up the stairs and up the aerial ladders, and keep up with the younger men. It isn't that one can't do it, it just becomes harder. Naturally, an older, experienced firefighter has the knowledge and wisdom of having fought countless fires and clearly, that is extremely important, but from a physical standpoint, the job is much more demanding on the body. A young man can take a beating on the night tour after a couple of fires, and go to bed. As you get older, it takes a couple of days to recover from the same beating.

It is documented that the life expectancy of a firefighter is about seven years after retirement. Most firefighters' bodies have been subjected to countless toxins, from smoke and chemicals. The physical abuse is well noted. Several firefighters leave with retirement disabilities like cancer and heart problems. As I prepared to end my twenty-six years of fighting fires in New York City with having survived the collapse of both World Trade Center towers, I wondered how well my body would endure. Many of the toxins that permeated the air that day remain unidentified, and thus, undocumented.

And yet, in spite of all of that – the wear and tear, the dangers, the long-term effects of the job - deep down, it was still difficult, as it is for many firefighters, to retire. Only when someone has been through the process can he understand what it means to be totally disconnected from this family. Continued association with old friends is wonderful, but it's not the same as actively working together.

A month earlier, I had visited my former company, Rescue 1, in Manhattan, to meet an old friend. I introduced myself to the house watchman as a former firefighter from the company. "Cap, I know exactly who you are. Come on in," the firefighter said. "There's some coffee in the back." It made me feel good that someone still knew me, but this was the sort of experience I wouldn't be having any more.

In addition to having to give up that second family, I was also leaving a career that I'd always felt had made my hard-working parents proud. Equally disturbing was the question I had begun to ask myself more and more: was there going to be anything else that I could do as well. People were encouraging and kind, saying things like, "Al, you're smart. You can do a lot," but I still wondered. Fear of the unknown exacerbated my self-doubts. More than anything, however, I just didn't want to cut the cord with my brothers who'd made the supreme sacrifice that day of 9/11.

And yet, things were changing; they had already changed. Because of the mass exodus of so many firefighters, officers and chiefs, many of the present firefighters, even after this short span of time, had not been in the department and experienced the attacks of 9/11. They didn't personally know, nor were they influenced by, the wonderful brave firefighters who died there. Ironically, they may have been motivated to join the department by these men and their example, just as I was by the bomberos, when I was that eight year old boy living on 99th Street in Harlem, but changes had been set in motion by a force beyond our control.

And so, I went to F.D.N.Y. Headquarters at 9 Metro Tech that winter morning, to return my F.D.N.Y. badge and I.D. In the badge office, two civilians were there to handle the paper work. One greeted me. "Can we help you?"

"I'm retiring," I told them "I'm here to hand in my badge and I.D."

"Can you give me your I.D.?" he asked.

I did so, and he placed it under a press. After the press had come down on it, he handed it back to me. I could see that my I.D. now had several perforations over my photo. I put it up towards the light and read, "RETIRED." That hit home. I didn't want to hand in my badge.

"If you want, since you have over twenty five years of service, you can buy your badge and retain your number," he said.

I paid twenty-five dollars for my badge and number: 1179. If, in the future, my son Matthew or a relative decides he wants to go into the F.D.N.Y., I would like to give him my badge.

After more than twenty five years of service, this was the way it all ended. How ironic, I thought. The moment was quick, uneventful and extremely sad. Nobody was with me, and that was good, but I felt lonely and empty. Not only had 9/11 robbed me of the person I was; it had now forced me to give up a part of my life.

When I got home, I didn't want to talk to anybody, because I felt they would say, "Come on, you have to get over it." I wanted to "get over it." No one enjoys feeling like a half broken-down human being, but it wasn't that simple. I had joined the F.D.N.Y. as a young man, and I wanted to talk about those days, about the friends and great individuals I'd met who had influenced both my career and my life, but I was afraid nobody would want to hear it. The next day, life goes on. That's it.

Now, with that winter morning receding into the past, I have the freedom to think about how I would like things to be. In the future, I'd like to get together with some close friends and sit in a bar where we'll act silly. We'll sing a couple of songs, tell some stories about the past, remember, and then toast all the brothers who aren't here with us anymore. Maybe we'll shed a tear or two; then we'll hug and take a cab home.

CHAPTER TWENTY-SEVEN

REFLECTIONS

I think mentally I'm doing extremely well. One of the sayings that I like to live by is, "Eventually, we all have to look in the mirror and hope we like what we see." Ultimately, we have to judge how we've used our lifetime and determine the character we've developed. On 9/11, I did what I believed was the right thing to do, and fortunately, I can look in the 'mirror' and live with myself. After the South Tower collapsed, I didn't flee the area, I stayed with my men. I've always wished I could have done more.

About a week before 9/11, I had gone to Ray Downey's office, Special Operations on Roosevelt Island, to discuss the possibility of bringing scuba diving to the Marine Division for the summer months, since we now had our faster smaller rescue boats. As I walked into his office, I noticed that Ray had a quotation hanging on his wall by Theodore Roosevelt that my children and I have had posted in our rooms for years, and that I'm sure many firefighters have as a slogan. It reads: "It is not the critic who counts; not the man who points out how the strong man stumbled, or where the doer of deeds could have done them better. The credit belongs to the man who is actually in the arena, whose face is marred by dust and sweat and blood; who strives valiantly; who errs and comes short again and again, because there is no effort without error and shortcoming; but who does actually strive to do the deeds; who knows the great enthusiasms, the great devotions; who spends himself in a worthy cause; who at the best knows in the end the triumph of high achievement, and who at worst, if he fails, at least fails while daring greatly, so that his place shall never be with those cold and timid souls who know neither victory nor defeat."

This was the 'arena' that we were thrown into on September 11th, 2001. I believe Roosevelt's description of the "man who is actually in the arena" embodies the 343 firefighters, rescuers and all the civilians who died in that arena. Their actions showed the world that leadership, bravery and commitment to life were what they believed in.

Ray Downey's sons Joe and Chuckie bestowed a great honor on me. Both are following in the footsteps of their father as firefighters, Joe as a Battalion Chief and Chuckie, a Captain. When they visited me at my home, they asked if I would write and deliver the eulogy for their father at the memorial mass that was to be held for him. I was deeply moved by their request. It truly was an honor to talk about my friend, not only as a leader in our firefighting vocation but as the truly wonderful human being he was, a loving husband and father and a true and loyal friend.

After 9/11, I always thought I'd have several dreams about that day. The initial nightmare that I had in the hospital, of the poor innocent civilian workers jumping from the Towers, occurred when the doctors were weaning me off the drugs that had kept me in the coma. I had hoped that I would have other dreams, that I might go back, if even for just a minute in time, to see and talk to my brothers, but I've had only two. I wish to pass them on to you.

My first dream was of Pete Ganci. I was driving through my old hometown of Woodside. On the corner of 58th Street and Woodside Avenue is St. Sebastian's grammar school which I attended and where the Boys' Brigade meetings were held. A short distance away, there is a beautiful monument dedicated to the many men from my neighborhood who died in the Vietnam War. As I drove past it in my dream, I noticed Pete standing across from it. I couldn't believe my eyes - my friend, brother and leader. I quickly pulled over, got out and walked toward him with my arms opened wide. Pete opened his and we hugged. I knew he had died, and he knew too. I proceeded to tell him how much the department and I missed him. I asked if he was all right. "Uncle Al," he said, with that small defining smile he always had, "I'm doing great. I'm happy." We started walking towards the monument and he continued to talk, while I listened. "But I'm worried about the brothers down there," he said. "They're truly hurting. Please tell them we're fine." As we reached the monument, he continued to walk past the school, and we departed. I woke up and called his wife, Cathy.

My second dream was with Ray Downey, whom I had wanted so desperately to talk to and see again. One night, I finally did. We were in a lobby of a hotel. Many people were around, and I sensed that we were at a response type meeting, the kind we'd taken part in, so many times before. Ray was himself, giving orders, telling people what he expected, covering all the bases. I just kept staring at him, as I didn't want to lose sight of his beautiful face. I'd missed him so much and had thought of him daily, since 9/11. He finally noticed me and came over. We made some small talk, and he proceeded to explain some jobs that he wanted me to take care of.

After he finished, he looked at me and said, "Okay Al, thanks, and take care of that for me, please." "Consider it done, Pal," I said. He started walking away, and so did I. Suddenly, I realized that I might never see him again, so I turned and called after him, "Ray." We began walking back toward each other, and he looked directly into my eyes. I slowly raised my hand and touched his right cheek. "Ray, have I ever told you that I loved you?" I said. He turned slowly to his right, looked up and seemed as if he were trying to understand what I'd just said. And then, I woke up.

CHAPTER TWENTY-EIGHT

A VIEW TO THE FUTURE

It has been more than two years since 9/11 and the attacks on the World Trade Center, but sometimes it feels as if it happened yesterday. At the same time, I still have difficulty comprehending its magnitude and the fact that I survived. Every day, I think of my brother firefighters, the rescuers and the civilians who lost their lives, especially those who jumped to their deaths. Their faces and the scenes of that morning are deeply etched into my mind. I wake with them, and I go to bed with them. Sometimes, I still wake up in the middle of the night and expect to find Ray or Pete standing next to my bed. They're not there, but I do feel them near me.

When I rise in the morning now, I pray and thank God that I have one more day. That's the way I look at life now, a day at a time, some days good, others less so; mostly, they're good, and their memories reoccupy my consciousness.

In this final chapter, I hope to touch upon three major issues that continue to distress me, in light of what occurred on September 11th, 2001, but I don't wish to end there. I would like to close with a vision of the future, my own and ours.

By now, many of my injuries have healed, and some never will. The damage to my lungs continues its destructive course. For the sake of economy, I will focus on just this one injury. Over a year and a half ago, I had agreed to have a special test performed on my lungs at Montefiore Hospital; the samples were then wired to a lab in Texas. There, it was confirmed that my lungs had tested positive for a significant amount of asbestos, various chemicals and other contaminants combined with the WTC dust that consisted of ground glass and other toxic materials. As a result of these findings, and in order for me to be able to have a record, I requested that a CAT scan be performed. A second CAT scan was performed a year later, again at my request, but this one was met with some resistance from the F.D.N.Y. I was retired now, they argued, and objected to the cost.

This second scan indicated similar results to the earlier: damage to the lower section of both lungs and the presence of numerous nodules; however, one important difference was significant growth in one of the nodules. The doctors at NYU advised that a third scan be performed in three months, in order for them to observe whether or not the growth of the nodule was continuing, and at what pace. They would then decide if a biopsy would be necessary to determine the presence of any malignancy. I wanted to be able to be seen by the best doctors, but the F.D.N.Y. reiterated that since I was retired, they would no longer cover those medical expenses; my family carrier also denied coverage, saying that my claims were based on previous existing injuries.

I was irate. I explained to the F.D.N.Y. physicians that when the South Tower collapsed, I didn't flee. "I stayed with my men," I told them, "and I expect the F.D.N.Y. to stay with me now, and assist me in dealing with the injuries that I incurred on that day."

I find it shocking that the department can so easily abrogate its responsibility and dispose of us, once we're no longer useful. I strongly believe that they should be responsible for ensuring that everyone in my situation not only receive the best medical care possible, but that the department should cover these and all future related medical expenses. Since this issue was not meeting with any resolution, and my concern was only increasing, I decided on a course of action. Presently, a law firm has offered to take my case on a pro-bono basis.

Another disturbing issue of the aftermath of September 11th concerns all of those who found a way of capitalizing on the blood of my brothers. A few of these 'entrepreneurs' – some of them firefighters – responded with pen, paper and camera rather than digging tools, when they went to 'assist' in the recoveries at Ground Zero. They wrote books and still conduct seminars around the country. They're a disgrace to the men and women who sacrificed their lives, and a disgrace to the real rescuers who came to assist on that morning, and on all the mornings, afternoons and evenings of that whole long year, without any thought as to monetary reward.

The abuse of free trips and gifts that were offered by well-meaning individuals and companies trying to assist the actual victims and their families, after the tragedy, was another concern. One can always find a reason, I guess, to accept trips and gifts, but many individuals became obsessed, and continued to put their names on lists that would make them available for these trips, family vacations, baseball games, free gifts and more.

In reality, there weren't many of these self-serving individuals. They were greatly outnumbered by the selfless and heroic rescuers and civilians alike who showed America by their example, what being American is all about. These people inspired patriotism and brought it to levels that I hadn't seen in my lifetime, making us so proud of who we were.

While I was recuperating at home, my friend, now retired, Pete Lund from Rescue 2, visited me, and as we sat in the backyard, he told me that the Gordon Bennett medal, the highest award given in the F.D.N.Y., didn't mean that much to him anymore. He said, "What I saw that day and the days afterward during the rescue efforts at Ground Zero was amazing." He went on to explain how he had witnessed young, old, retired firefighters, police officers, EMS and civilians alike, conducting themselves in ways that at any time could have warranted medals. "They were all Gordon Bennett medal winners," performing acts of bravery in situations so unstable and dangerous that it was wonderful to watch. I remember his message brought tears to my eyes. I've never forgotten this.

Another group that goes unnoticed are all the older retired firefighters who were either away or otherwise physically unable to help in the rescue efforts. It's well known by everyone that the retired members, as well as Americans throughout the nation, shared the grief of the victims' families and rescuers alike. People just wanted to be here and do what they could, but many couldn't. I've met with some of those firefighters and others who have felt inadequate about that time, and I wish to tell them all that they were with us.

A final issue, one that concerns all of us, is the situation that existed and changes that must be made. I've said many times in conversation that on 9/11, all of us - both rescuers and civilians in the Towers - were dead men walking. As rescuers, we responded and performed our jobs, as this was our duty and our commitment to this Department and the citizens of New York City. The F.D.N.Y. and the rescuers were responsible for the greatest rescue performed in the civilized world. Over 25,000 people were evacuated and saved.

While the F.D.N.Y. suffered a staggering death toll of 343 firefighters, other departments in the city suffered their own share of casualties, not in such high numbers perhaps, but equal in the pain such losses entail. The death toll will most certainly increase in years to follow, as a result of the exposure to all that the rescuers and workers at Ground Zero were vulnerable to.

The fact remains that the F.D.N.Y. must change now, and embrace the ever evolving and updated technology that will prove useful in preventing loss of lives. As of yet, it has not.

An example that comes to mind – and there are many – is the way the command post presently maintains a record of the companies that respond and are operating at fires or emergencies. This vital tracking method consists of a small folding table and magnetic pieces that represent the individual fire companies and their arrival sequence. Their job assignments are then noted by putting their corresponding magnet (company I.D.) on top of the board that is marked in crayon to represent the building, floors or area in question. Should the table fall, magnets drop, and I.D.'s of companies and their important locations are lost, as happened on 9/11. There was a fatal fire in Brooklyn a few years back, at which we lost three firefighters in the collapse of a multi-family frame building. There was no indication as to who the trapped members were, or where they were, and therefore, rescue efforts were hampered.

Technology could benefit this department in so many areas. One example is a chip that could be inserted inside all the radios (HT) of all members and officers, then digitally activated at the fire scene. Now, the officers in charge of the emergency operation would be better able to electronically and safely maintain a tracking of the movement of all firefighters in these buildings and dangerous situations, at a display in the thus updated command post. Now, should the immediate need arise, they would be able to zoom in on them, determine their exact location (which is automatically updated for any movement) for extrication and rescue efforts. Instead, as has been well-documented by the media, we continue to work with inferior radios that did, could and will continue to become vital in time of emergency.

There are countless other issues that the administration should be seeking to rectify and make improvements, and I can only ask, how long does it take? Do you really believe these are the best radios available, or is money the issue? We could talk to astronauts on the moon, thirty-five years ago, but ask us to talk to other firefighters in danger of losing their lives thirty floors above in a high-rise or underneath in a subway, and we can't. It's clear that the administration is trying to address some of these issues, but these are only a fraction of the many needed to secure the safety of our first responders in this new war. The clock is ticking, and we need answers now. Communication is one of the first areas we must address.

We live in a new world. The possibility of another even greater terrorist attack, is a matter of *when* not *if.* I still vividly recall the collapse of the South Tower, and my initial disbelief that all 110 floors collapsed in that cascading pancake into sixteen acres of rubble, in a matter of eight to ten seconds. We had anticipated a partial and gradual collapse of the entire area above the impact zone, but in all my twenty-six years of experience with F.D.N.Y. and with FEMA, I would never have predicted this type of total catastrophic collapse, not even after the building's being struck by a large commercial airliner with thousands of gallons of burning jet fuel. In my mind, as an experienced emergency officer, the basic construction of the World Trade Center was inherently faulty, and doomed for failure.

It is a well-known fact that because the Port Authority had built the WTC Towers, it was able to by-pass the more stringent New York City building codes. Individual floor areas, in order to accommodate more office space and generate more rents, were approximately 40,000 square feet of open unobstructed floor space. I believe that eventually there would have been a large volume of fire in the upper floors, which the F.D.N.Y. would not have been able to extinguish or control. It would have communicated to various floors above. With the inherently faulty sprayed-on fire protection of the structural steel beams, those beams would have failed. And this scenario would have had disastrous results, with a major, if not total collapse and possibly thousands of casualties.

These types of high-rise buildings continue to be built without any consultations with the F.D.N.Y. and other safety agencies. For the sake of space, I would cite a few situations that make these buildings extremely dangerous for occupancy. First, the fire department has long realized that a safe living/working space must have at least two means of egress, and that they must be remote, in relation to each other; in addition, these exits should be constructed of durable and fire resistant materials (i.e. concrete), not just two pieces of sheetrock that have met a laboratory test in a controlled environment.

Exits in the WTC Towers were situated around (in close proximity to each other) the core area, in the center of the buildings, where the elevator shafts ran, in order to minimize space usage and have more open office space. However, in one isolated case, because of structural issues in the building of one of the towers, there was one exit that was built and situated remote from the core area of the building and the other exits. It is from this independent exit that four civilians, the only ones known to have escaped from above both of the impact areas of the planes, were able to evacuate and save their lives. I strongly believe this fact speaks volumes.

Another situation that I find disturbing concerns the evacuation of the special populations: handicapped, elderly, young, medically impaired, and the special needs individuals, such as pregnant women. Accessibility is no problem, as far as entering these buildings is concerned, but in times of an emergency, such as the WTC attacks, what then? Who is responsible? How will they evacuate? Who will assist them before the first responders arrive? Elevators are shut down, as they are inferiorly constructed and oftentimes, extremely unsafe (yet another issue). Is this population to be put aside while the more ambulatory are allowed to evacuate?

Sadly, but true, many of these people died on September 11th, because of their inability to evacuate rapidly. Many rescuers and good-Samaritan civilians died alongside them. Are the 'refuge' areas that are to hold these special populations until all others evacuate, structurally safe? The total collapse of the WTC Towers, again speaks volumes.

I am angered to think that this dangerous situation continues to exist all around our great nation and that nothing is really being done about it. As I write this, architects, engineers, and developers are trying to address some of these problems; they're scrambling to figure out how to deal with them. I've heard some of these ideas, like providing an area of refuge with sprinklers, double sheetrock (again) and other nice "lab tested" materials, all inexpensive ways of solving the problem on paper. But these problems and others like them need real answers with consultations with a variety of professionals who have experience in all the different disciplines. We must prepare to properly and safely protect our citizens and assist our first responders in the ever changing, highly dangerous emergencies to which they will be called.

We were all witnesses to a most wonderful and generous outpouring of love and support from all Americans during and after this disaster. Through my association with the families of many of my brothers who made the supreme sacrifice, I have been able to witness the monetary generosity that has been bestowed on these families, through the many charities and funds that were created. The great personal loss of their loved ones will always remain, but because of this over-whelming generosity, some of their stress has been mini-mized; at least, a small part of their lives can be taken care of, and they can move forward. On my Brothers' behalf, I wish to personally thank all the millions of people who have helped these families in their time of need. Stories abound about all the different ways that Americans – communities, businesses and individuals alike – have gathered together to find ways to contribute.

As an adolescent growing up in Woodside, I would hear the older men in our neighborhood talk about World War II and the Korean War. These veterans would say things like, "all of our past war veterans fought for us to enjoy the freedoms that we have today," and I admit that as a teenager, I really thought many of their statements were exaggerated and sometimes, untrue. After having lived through September 11th, 2001 and witnessed how innocent civilians and first responders valiantly died, I have now come to realize, like those older men of my boyhood, that freedom does not come free. It is earned and defended by our soldiers and now, by our first responders. We are indebted to them.

During a recent visit to San Francisco, I was given a tour of the Silver Oaks winery in Napa Valley. Here, a wonderful man, an ex-marine and now a deacon, named Bob, reenacted for my wife Eileen and me, how he lovingly played TAPS on 9/12/01, in honor of the thousands who had died in the attacks on the WTC, Washington and Pennsylvania. He played the trumpet from inside a stainless steel, cylindrical, vacant vat, ordinarily used to ferment the wine. The sound that drifted out was heavenly, surreal, probably the most mystical TAPS I have ever heard. Eileen and I and our friends who were present were brought to tears. This same gentleman then wrote me a thank-you and inside his letter, he wrote,

> "To be born free is an accident, to live free is a privilege, to die free is a responsibility."   Deacon Bob

When I read his note, 9/11 flashed inside my mind. I have always maintained that we saw the worst and the best in humanity that day. I choose to remember the best. While the F.D.N.Y. suffered staggering losses, I believe it was our finest hour; in fact, it was the finest hour for all firefighters in our nation, and they represented what is best in all Americans.

America is far from ideal. We have many faults, and we have suffered greatly many times for these faults. It isn't my intention to say that America is perfect; it is far from that. It is however, the land that I love and that I have chosen to make my family's and my home. My mother Aida and father Alfredo have endured and suffered much, in making America their home. My brother Rick also made great sacrifices to help our family. I owe it to them and all the immigrants before me to be the best I can.

We citizens of this country, many from other lands, have come to a crossroads in our country's ever-changing journey and we need to make a decision. Are we Americans, or are we not? We cannot continue to just enjoy its freedoms, financial benefits and safety, and not be completely sure that this is where we want to live. It is time to stop merely complaining about what is wrong and instead, become part of the solution. I know it sounds harsh and finite, but I strongly believe that if we affirm our love to our country as my brothers did, we will have gone a long way toward beginning to address some of the problems that affect our nation and the world. I hope that as a society, we understand and come to accept that Americans come in all sizes, shapes and colors, and that we speak several different languages.

As for me ... I plan to continue healing and learning to enjoy a sunrise, a laugh, a hug from my wife and children, every once in a while. I hope to see my grandchildren, and I hope to be able to assist my fellow firefighters and first responders in their mission and ever-changing, dangerous job. I plan to wear my patriotic pin and fly my flag. And one day, when I'm gone and with my firefighting brothers in a better world, assisting them in putting out the fires in hell, I hope that someone will remember how so many sacrificed their lives, and how all of us as Americans responded, in that moment of need, to our fellow human beings.

PART FOUR
EYEWITNESS ACCOUNTS

F.D.N.Y. FIREFIGHTER JOHN COLON

My name is John Colon. I have been a New York City fireman for over twenty years. I live on Staten Island, New York. On the morning of September 11th, 2001, I was at home on vacation. At the time, I was assigned to Ladder 103 in the East New York section of Brooklyn. My wife and I had just walked our three year old daughter to her first day of pre-school, returned home and were in our yard when we heard an explosion. Although we didn't know what it was, I told my wife it didn't sound good. A few minutes later, when we went into the house and my wife put on the television, we saw the World Trade Center on fire. At the time, we weren't certain if we were witnessing the second building's being struck or if we were watching a replay. I immediately gathered my second set of fire gear and reported to the firehouse closest to where I live, which is Engine 159. I made a journal entry and went with another fireman to the Staten Island ferry. We boarded and waited for it to depart.

All the while, we were watching the upper floors of the North Tower burning and had no sight of the second tower. I couldn't believe that a building of that size would come down, and I expected to see it at some point behind Tower One, when we got into the Hudson River on our way to Manhattan.

We waited at the ferry for what seemed like a long time. We were waiting for firefighters, police and EMS workers to board, so that we could leave with a full boat.

We were almost in Manhattan when we witnessed Tower One, the remaining tower, come down. When we arrived, we walked to the Trade Center via the promenade which runs along the river, and when we got close to West Street, I noticed an injured Battalion Chief coming out of the rubble. We had worked together in Ladder 103. When we reached West Street, we received a call for help from a fireman who was giving maydays on the radio. At this time, I saw nothing but burning rigs and rubble and although it was morning, it felt as if day were night, from all the dust and debris.

As we went searching for this fireman who was sending the distress radio calls, two firemen who were directly in front of me found him. Al was lying on a beam. I realized that he was critically injured and in a lot of pain. He was complaining about his back, and he had frothy blood coming out of his mouth and was having difficulty breathing. I knew he had lung problems. All I could do for him at that point was hold his hand and give him encouragement and tell him that he was going to be okay. We were trying to figure out the best way to remove this large man from the rubble.

I noticed two firemen approaching the scene from opposite directions and I asked one of them to go back and try to find a stretcher or stokes carrier, which is used to carry injured victims. I asked the other fireman to help us find the easiest way to get Al to a safe point from which he could then be transported. While we waited for the two firemen to return, we cut Al's bunker pants off. There was very little else that we could do for him until we got the stokes. After a few minutes, one of the men came back with the stokes, and as we were packaging Al up, the other returned with the good news that he'd found a way to transport him through one of the buildings and to the safety of a New York City fireboat which would then transport him to where he could receive medical attention.

After a couple of minutes, more firemen arrived. It took nine of us to carry Al. It was extremely difficult for us to get our footing as we carried him through rubble consisting of metal beams and twisted steel. As one of us would lose our footing and fall into the rubble, the next man would take his place. We continued until we got him out. When we reached the marina, we put Al, accompanied by Terry Jordan, on a New York City Fire Department boat and transported him to a hospital in New Jersey.

I didn't know if Al had survived or not. I was very happy to know that he was still alive when we put him on that boat. Leaving him while he was still alive helped me through that day. Al was the only survivor whom I came across in the rubble that day.

We'd gotten to the Trade Center around eleven a.m. and I wasn't able to get in touch with my wife until about three p.m. No one knew whether or not I was alive. I didn't get home until four p.m. on September 12th.

After about a week, I found out for the first time that Al had survived and was in critical condition. After a few months, I heard that he had been released from the hospital, and we made arrangements to meet at my firehouse in East New York, Brooklyn. I told him about my experience with him on that day. I gave him the picture of us carrying him out of the rubble. If there was anything that has helped me through my experience of September 11th, it was finding Al alive, which was truly a miracle.

F.D.N.Y. LIEUTENANT TOM HAUGHNEY

Six months before 9/11, I had been promoted from Fireman to Lieutenant. Normally, new lieutenants get promoted and go to a different division. This time some of us had to go offline for a year and serve in an administrative position. It was a low point in my career because I did not want administrative duties. I'm a firefighter.

I had been assigned to the Preventive Maintenance Division. I was in a box performing the routine of scheduling oil changes at the Rock (The Fire Academy). There were a couple of other new lieutenants at the Rock, while other new lieutenants went to the FDNY Headquarters in Brooklyn for other administrative positions. That's how I ended up being at the Academy on 9/11.

THE MORNING OF 9/11

I was in the office that morning waiting for rigs to come in to get oil changes. I would get in there early and the rigs would come in after 9 A.M. A friend of mine, who had gotten promoted with me, was in the next building over at the Mask Service Unit.

Some mechanics told me that a plane had hit the World Trade Center. When I looked outside my window, I could see the tower smoking. I told mechanics, "I'm going to run over to the Mask Service Unit where my friend is. I know they have a television in the lounge."

Sure enough, my friend and others were watching everything unfold on TV. We wondered if a small plane had accidentally flown into the tower. We didn't think there was much we could do because we were on administrative detail. After I went back to my office, my father, who is a retired firefighter, called me up and asked, "Have you seen the events that are going on? I've been listening to the scanner."

As soon as I heard another plane had hit the second tower, I ran back to the Mask Service Unit. I caught up with my friend and said, "I'm just going to go on down there. I want to see if I can help." I had no idea what I could do.

I ran back to the office to get ready to go. My father had called a second time. After talking to him, I said, "I'm planning to go down on my own." All maintenance schedules were cancelled immediately. I had access to the deputy chiefs' cars that were there for maintenance, so I told the mechanics, "I'm taking one of the deputy chief's car. I'm heading down there."

One of the light duty firefighters, who was assigned to drive the rigs for maintenance, said, "I'll go with you."

We got in a deputy chief's car and were near Building 9, which is the main headquarters, near the front of the Rock. I saw another friend of mine, Captain Mike Woods, handing out the SCBA masks (masks with air) and radios. I noticed a bus filling up with assembled firefighters and officers, so I pulled over.

"Mike, what are you doing?" I asked my friend.

"We're all going down there on the bus," he said.

I thought it best to go along with them and take along a radio and mask, rather than drive down on my own. I told the other light duty firefighter who had just had surgery on his bad knees, "Stay back. I'll go with these guys."

I got out and jumped on the bus. It couldn't have been more crowded. I made eye contact with my friend in the Mask Service Unit. I hadn't realized that he was coming, but he was there in the front. We wondered aloud what we were going to come upon, at this scene. I walked past him and found one seat left in the back.

Someone got on and yelled, "One of the buildings came down," and I thought he meant part of the top had collapsed. I never imagined a whole building could come down.

Chief Santangelo, the Chief of Training, was the last to get on. There was no more room on the bus. The adrenaline was running and everyone started screaming, "Pull out! Let's go! Let's go!"

As we went over the Triborough Bridge, we could see one building still standing and in flames. There were a lot of emotions on the bus. People were screaming, "Who did this? We have to get these guys!" I continued to wonder, what kind of scene I would come upon.

I looked to the men around me and kept thinking it's ten minutes to nine; there's going to be twenty thousand people in there. What are we going to do? All we can do is calm down, get down there, and see. If I can only help one person, I thought, that's what I'll do. After that, I'll help another, I decided. I didn't want to get overwhelmed before I even got to the scene.

As we drove down, someone was writing down names of those on the bus and organizing us into groups. I had made it a point to stay with my captain friend. I said, "Mike, let's just you and I plan on staying together, if nothing else." He and I knew some firefighters on the bus who were at the academy for chauffeur training school at the time, so about five of us grouped together.

We were in a converted school bus that had been painted red. The police had been very good about closing off the bridges and tunnels. We drove down the FDR on the East Side and it was mostly vacant.

As we got to Lower Manhattan, we saw thousands of people walking north on the highway. They were covered in dust from the building's collapse and looked like a group of zombies that one would see in a movie.

We came around the Battery Park Tunnel of Lower Manhattan and up West Street. As we pulled up, the second building came down. Our visibility was obscured again. We had air masks, but the masks were good for only eleven minutes. They were purified air masks. They call them 30-minute cylinders, but they're good for 11 minutes of operation before an alarm goes off that tells you you have six more minutes of air. I had this mask on my back the whole time, but I never used it because I knew I was going to be there for a long operation. When the bus stopped, I popped open the emergency door in the back. There was a sudden rush of smoke and dust inside the bus. Fifty of us started scrambling off.

On West Street, there were two walking bridges. The north side had crashed onto the street, which kept any units from the north from responding on West Street. We had come in from the south and parked just before the south walking bridge which was still intact.

We were the first ones on the scene after the second collapse. It looked like a ghost town. There was no one to be found. All we could hear were explosions from car fires and tires popping from the heat. All the tall buildings around us were completely engulfed in fire.

Chief Santangelo had us break off into groups. There was so much fire I hardly knew where to begin. We checked and found there was no water. The hydrants and water mains had been broken from the collapse. The chief wanted to get a hose line into operation. He had asked us to get a manifold because they were planning on drafting water from the Hudson River.

We hadn't brought any equipment on the bus, so we had to search for equipment. A lot of companies had pulled up with their fire engines prior to the collapse and had gone in. We were looking for fire engines that had equipment on them – manifolds, hoses. We managed to find one manifold and reported it to Chief Santangelo.

"Listen. There's a report of a captain who's down. We think he's around here on West Street," Chief Santangelo told us.

I was expecting to find thousands of injured people. I found no injured. Once we heard about the captain being down, we said, "O.K. We're going to drop everything and get him."

My goal of helping one person and then another flashed before me.

The six of us fanned out and started to search. We made our way through the rubble in a straight line. As best we could, we headed up what had been West Street toward the north walking bridge.

We came upon fire trucks and fire engines. Some were buried and others were unrecognizable. As we looked in the rubble, we would come across a diamond plate. After closer evaluation, I would say, "This is a fire truck. I can't believe this is a fire truck."

We tried to check the cabs for firefighters in there, but no one was there. We would rub off the dust on the truck curious to see what company it was. We kept climbing over the rubble that was several stories high. There were fires and smoke everywhere around us.

About forty minutes later, the firefighter to the left of me said, "I think I see a coat!" This firefighter was pointing between us. As we got closer we saw a stripe on his sleeve from his fire coat. I climbed over the rubble and I saw it was the captain, buried face down. I had never met Captain Al Fuentes before this.

Ironically, my father had been listening at home on his scanner and had heard the captain calling for help to the city-wide dispatcher. Only head and shoulders were visible. He was covered with dust and then I saw that his scalp had been torn back off his head.

THE RESCUE

The other firefighters searching came right over. Mike Woods, the captain, who was to my right, came over. "Cap, we're here," I said to Captain Fuentes. "Your head is pretty badly cut. Is there anything else that really hurts?" I asked. We were going to try to free him and I did not want to jostle him, if he had broken bones. "My back," Al managed to mumble. He had part of the façade from the building across his back in addition to all the rubble. I radioed to Chief Santangelo, "We found the captain. We need a stokes basket or a stretcher. We're starting to extricate him."

When we radioed that we had found him, it seemed like all operations focused on getting Al out, as other firefighters arrived. Everyone wanted to help. Al was the first and only person who had been uncovered. Everyone focused on and channeled his energy into freeing the captain.

I got on the far end of the piece of the façade that was hanging across him. Another firefighter had a halligan, which is basically a three-foot long piece of iron used as a pry bar. We wedged the halligan against the façade. As the façade was lifted up by a firefighter, another firefighter and I grabbed Al under the arms and we tried to lift him. He didn't move. We cleared some more debris off him and Mike Woods got his feet free from under the debris. Then another firefighter and I grabbed him under the armpits and we dragged him straight out. I turned my mask on and helped the face piece down onto his face to see if he wanted some purified air. He pushed it away with his hands. He wasn't speaking, but I knew he didn't want it.

THE STOKES (WIRE MESH) BASKET ARRIVES

Other firefighters came with a stokes basket, so we lifted him and then put him in it. There was another chief who said, "Probably the best way to get him out from here is to get him on one of the fireboats. We'll get him to a hospital from the river." Our plan was to take him across West Street, go through one of the buildings, and out to the fireboat on the Hudson River.

We had a major problem getting him over the rubble that was several stories high. There were no shortcuts for carrying this man on a stretcher. We would inch him over a mound, step over the rubble, and drag him a little further. The brothers were climbing ahead over the rubble and yelling, "Pass him along!" As soon as one guy passed the feet, he would run ahead and try to carry him a little farther.

Al had been placed almost face down on his right side. We didn't have any collars or any way to stabilize him. His head was badly cut, but fortunately it was full of the concrete dust that kept him from bleeding to death. I know one firefighter had his glove over his head trying to keep pressure on his head. Al lay on his right side, and I was at his back, near his belt. I told myself, I'm not going to let go of this guy until we get him on the boat.

With his left hand, Al was patting the arm of the guys holding the other side of the stokes basket. It was touching because it was Al's way of saying, "Thanks a lot for getting me out of here." Otherwise, Al was not coherent. He was not speaking, but he remained semi-conscious. I was amazed to see he had the wherewithal to thank the firefighters helping to carry him out.

As we inched along, guys were starting to lose their grip. Out of exhaustion, the guys would say, "Put him down! I'm going to drop him." Other guys would say, "No way! No way! We're not stopping! We're taking this guy." There were a number of guys who were helping, even if it was only carrying the stokes basket a couple of feet over the rubble. It was really a team effort.

I started saying, "I'm exhausted! We've got to rest." Other guys insisted, "No! We're going to do it!" We rallied and kept him moving along over the mounds of debris, inching ourselves all the way to the fireboat.

It wasn't until we could pass through a large broken plate glass window on the ground floor of one of the buildings that we could hustle him along. We went into some office and from there, down what seemed to be a maze of long hallways. The brothers were great. Firefighters were forcing doors open. The guys would run ahead and open doors for us as we carried him out. At one point, we even had to go down an escalator that was no longer operational and then came out on the promenade at the water. We reached the gangplank that leads to the fireboat. It was so narrow that at that point, only two of us could fit and carry the stretcher.

A photographer had taken a picture of us carrying Al. In the picture, my face is obscured, but I can be partly identified by the edge of my new Lieutenant's front piece. That's exactly how I prefer it.

We got him to the side of the fireboat and some of the crew from the Marine Unit pulled him aboard. They placed him on the back of the fireboat and took off. We were exhausted. I said, "This is an unreal situation. Right now, we're going to have to go back and keep looking. We found one. Let's go find another."

When we were on our way back from the boat, I was coming through the American Express Building onto West Street again. Some other firefighters had found the chauffeur from 65 Engine. They had found him partially buried underneath the fire apparatus and were putting him in a stokes basket and carrying him out. I took a turn at carrying him over the rubble, but I came to the point at which I said, "I can't hold him anymore. I have to pass him off." We continued to search for the rest of the day and night.

Around five o'clock that night, Tower Seven, a forty-seven story building, collapsed after being consumed by fire the entire day. I felt that this collapse was ironic because the collapse of a forty-seven story building would have been a huge story, but today it was just a footnote. I stood there watching that building come down, and shortly after, I was taken by ambulance to St. Vincent's Hospital after collapsing from exhaustion and dehydration. The entire time down there I kept telling myself, "Don't get consumed by what has happened. Just help wherever you can. Help one person at a time." Al turned out to be the only person we found.

As I went home the next morning from the hospital, I thought about what a tragedy this was. Although we were expecting to be helping thousands, I helped only one person. I'm glad we saved Captain Fuentes, but I wish it could have been more. I've said to people, "There were two kinds of firefighters on 9/11: those who went home that day and those who didn't."

F.D.N.Y. LIEUTENANT TERRY JORDAN

I remember that morning because it was absolutely gorgeous. I was at the Fire Academy for our annual "Educational Day." All firefighters have to take turns away from their companies in order to spend a day at the Academy to refresh their skills. I was supposed to be working in Marine 9 that day, so Lieutenant Mickey McDonald filled in for me. While we were sitting in the cafeteria having a cup of coffee, we suddenly saw lots of officers running around. Everything was at high alert for some reason; it was obvious something serious was going on. Those of us there for Educational Day were called into a back room and told that a plane had hit one of the towers at the World Trade Center. I knew a fire in that location meant an automatic fifth alarm. That meant a lot of firefighters would be at the Trade Center. We were immediately released and told to report back to our assigned companies. When we heard what had happened, we began thinking this must be an act of terrorism.

Initially, we were going to go over to SOC headquarters (Special Operations Command) on Roosevelt Island. Once I realized the terrible traffic conditions, I thought we had a better chance of staying on the BQE (Brooklyn-Queens Expressway) and going to the Marine headquarters at the

Brooklyn Navy Yard.

There were police roadblocks everywhere. I was using my badge to get through the roadblocks, and I lost count as to how many there were. While driving, I heard over the radio that another plane had struck the second tower. That confirmed to me that it was terrorism.

As we were making our way to the Marine Division's headquarters, I witnessed the South Tower come down. I knew there were going to be several civilian fatalities, and that countless brother firefighters were in that building. A lot of emotions ran through me, but I had no idea that hundreds of my brothers had just died. The sense of urgency was so great, that I couldn't get there fast enough. People may not understand that about firefighters. They might wonder why firefighters came in from home. That's just our nature and our training, to want to respond in an emergency.

Along the way, I kept in contact by cell phone with the other firefighters who were following right behind me. When we arrived at our headquarters, we were told that Captain Fuentes had already responded to the World Trade Center. It appeared Lt. Traks was in charge of the Marine Division.

I decided to activate the "Smoke," which is the staff fireboat. It is not always in service and is usually used when another boat breaks down.

"Go upstairs. Empty out the CFR-D locker. Take everything we have and stow it on the boat," I told the crew. The CFR-D supplies are one step below paramedic supplies. A number of us were certified in using these supplies. I expected we would be performing emergency medical treatments ourselves on hundreds or thousands of victims with major medical traumas.

Lt. Traks directed us to stand fast in case there was another attack. The Marine 6 fireboat was standing fast on the

Brooklyn Bridge in the case of another attack.

I heard Captain Fuentes on the super radio. He called the dispatcher requesting help. Al is a friend of mine. I sensed the urgency of the situation. I did away with Lt. Traks' idea of sticking around, yelled to the crew, "Cast the lines," and we took off in the Smoke heading for the World Trade Center. I notified the Manhattan dispatcher we were heading over and that we would be coming in at the North Cove Marina. I prepped the crew by telling them, "We're going to see things that you never thought you would ever see in your life. We'll just have to ignore that and do our job."

I directed two of the pilots to act as communications coordinators and coordinate water supply. I figured that water mains would be out. In fact, we did supply seawater (the standard lingo for drafting water) for the first couple of days because the mains were not working.

On the way over, we heard that Al was near West Street and Vesey. That gave us a general idea where he might be. I asked for volunteers to help in the search. Everybody volunteered. I made up two teams to work the search. I could hear Al blacking out during his radio transmissions and he sounded very weak. He gave west of Vesey as a location. In an effort not to pin ourselves to that one location, I planned that we would start upwind of that and work down. The other team would work the other side of West Street.

Initially, the air was horrendous. Every once in a while, a wind would come and blow a clearing. We would see a structure of steel that looked like fingers sticking up. Then the dust would fill in the sky again.

GETTING TO AL

We were at the marina in a matter of minutes after the second tower came down. My two teams had split up. When my teams got to the World Financial Center building, I had my men make a quick surface search as we went through to the other side of the building. On our way, we had to make our way through a long narrow, dark hallway.

As we got to the piles of debris, the visibility was very poor. We heard massive chunks of concrete or steel falling around us. It was a surreal situation. There were a lot of emergency vehicles crushed or on fire. We found ourselves walking into choking, terrible smelling, dusty air and looking around at a scene of complete devastation. "Try to get into one of these ambulances and get me some medical equipment to help Al," I told my men. When we got to the debris field, we did not see anybody else around as we began our search operations. My team ran into a couple of other firefighters, John Colon from Ladder 103, whom I knew, and another firefighter. All of a sudden one of the firefighters yelled out, "Over here! Over here!" Al was partially buried, face down. His head and chest were visible, but the rest of him was covered with debris. A couple of other firefighters came over. It was a frantic situation.

I sent some men to get the CFR-D equipment to stabilize him, a long board for his back, and a stokes basket. I wasn't sure if Al was going to make it. There was a firefighter standing by us with a radio. I asked him for the radio to notify the dispatcher that we had found Al, because the calls were still coming over to find Captain Fuentes. The firefighter made the call himself.

We stabilized Al as best we could. He was wrapped in metal and all kinds of structural materials. We got his body clear and cut his shirt off. We cut his bunker pants off. His mouth was filled with what looked like a pound of gray concrete dust. Pt. Joe Gagliardi swept that out with his finger and washed it out with a bottle of water that he had found. Al was having a lot of difficulty breathing. He had serious signs of trauma. He was scalped. He was speaking and complaining about breathing, but he was not fully cognizant.

Before we moved him, I did a full CFR-D assessment. He was having trouble breathing on one side. I felt his broken ribs and I figured his lung was popped by one of the ribs. I had him laid on the long board on his right side where he felt more comfortable.

"Al, it's Terry. We're going to get you out of here. Don't worry," I kept telling him. We put him on a long board to stabilize his spine. Then we put him, while on the long board, into the stokes. At this point, more firefighters were coming onto the debris field. It was very tough carrying him. I never realized how big Al was. Until that day, I though he was an average size guy. And this wasn't like walking down the block. We were climbing over mounds of debris and I-beams that were several stories high. It was like climbing up and down mountains, while at the same time the debris was giving way under our feet. It was a very tough rescue, so we needed all the extra firefighters to help. Whenever a firefighter dropped away from the stokes because he had lost his footing, another firefighter would jump in to take his place. When a firefighter regained his footing, he would come back to help the others. The men were getting hurt on the way out. I took a fall on an I-beam and wound up with a neck injury.

We made our way through the same broken window we had come out of at the World Financial Center building, where the Atrium of the Winter Garden had collapsed. On the way back, we had to go through the same long dark hallway, and as we came out of the back of that building, we ran into Chief Siegel. He asked, "What's going on?"

"We've got Al. I'm putting him on the boat and taking him

somewhere remote," I said. I thought all the area hospitals, like St. Vincent's, were going to be inundated. I still had an image in my mind that there would be so many victims in the Manhattan hospitals that the victims would have to be left in the street on gurneys, so I made the decision to get Al to a hospital away from Manhattan that could see him right away. We continued down and got Al on the boat. Initially, I told the pilot to bring us back to the Navy yard. I notified Manhattan and Brooklyn dispatchers that we had Al Fuentes and to have an ALS (Advanced Life Support) unit waiting for us at the Navy Yard. At first, I had expected Al to be taken to a Brooklyn hospital. As we started on our way, we looked over and saw emergency units with lights flashing on the Jersey Shore. We decided right then that it might be a better idea to bring him to Jersey. I knew there was a fantastic trauma unit a few blocks from the Colgate clock. That would be faster and it appeared there were emergency medical people already there, so I notified people on the Jersey shore to have an ALS unit waiting for us.

We pulled up to the pier at the Colgate clock, and the emergency workers assisted in off loading Al. I assigned one of my men to act as a liaison and keep in touch with the Marine Division in case anything was needed; he would also provide updates on Al's condition.

As soon as Al was offloaded, we headed right back. I was telling the men once again, "We're going to find hundreds, if not thousands of casualties, injuries, fatalities."

Since Al had turned up very quickly, we expected to go back and find others just as quickly.

When we got back, I assigned key members of the crew to supply water. Everybody was coming in on recall, so we had almost the whole company there. We were taking turns going out in search teams. What surprised us was that no bodies were turning up, nothing. At first, we didn't even find body parts. I cannot believe Al survived amidst all those acres of devastation. Around him were massive structural steel beams. It seemed as if he was in the middle of an A-shape of these beams that had fallen around him.

The next 48 hours I worked in the debris looking for survivors. When the buildings collapsed, the whole command structure of the fire department was devastated. Several of our chiefs, rescue companies, and heavy-duty companies got killed. After they were killed, there was no command structure. Anybody who showed up randomly searched for victims. Eventually, a command structure started to form. That's when a grid of the whole area was created and we started a more uniform search. Once we started digging, we found primarily body parts, and it was that way for the remainder of the time there. It had become an all-or-nothing experience of devastation that came down to finding heads, hands, and legs. People had disappeared and we could only find small pieces. For the first few days, we kept holding out hope that we would find people alive in air pockets under the debris.

ONE BRIGHT SPOT

We went through a very difficult time for about a year, because our lives were consumed by all the memorial services and the sadness. I lost my cousin's husband, a retired detective who was working in security for Cantor Fitzgerald, and her brother who is my cousin, also died there while working in the Cantor Fitzgerald security department. Al's survival was the only bright spot in this horrendous incident. I understand that the doctors told Al that if he had not been found and taken to the hospital, he would have been a goner in another twenty minutes. When we first started searching at

Ground Zero, I expected to find the worst medical scenario. It was the worst scenario possible, but without the victims. I am fortunate that I have this one bright light of having helped rescue Al, because most of the firefighters who searched all the first week never found anybody.

JERSEY CITY FIRE DEPARTMENT
FIREFIGHTER MIKE RAZZOLI

I was sitting on a pier at the Hudson River with a police sergeant when the first plane hit the first tower. We wondered how that could have happened on such a beautiful day. When the second plane came by, we heard a loud roar. It seemed to be coming over the Statue of Liberty. It roared faster. When it hit the building, we saw a huge fireball.

Immediately, I went to headquarters. From there, I got involved in helping set up a triage center. Al was not brought to the triage center where I was. He was brought in at the Colgate clock at Liberty Park, while others were brought in at Hudson Street, at the ferry dock.

The chief did a recall. Right after the collapse, Chief Lovero from Jersey City had gone across the river to help along with another Jersey firefighter, Buck Weaver. There were many Jersey City firefighters jumping in boats and going over. My brother who is a Jersey City police officer went over. He was helping to search for survivors. The debris was so hot that his boots melted.

The chief was organizing a task force because our headquarters is right outside the Holland Tunnel. Later that day, firefighters and police would go into the Path train tunnel at the Exchange Station in New Jersey on rafts. The tunnel had flooded, so they tried for several days to pump water out.

MEETING AL IN THE HOSPITAL

I got burned in 1991 at a chemical fire. I'll never forget lying in that bed. It's a hard thing to be alone in the hospital. I remember being there and worrying about my family. Since I knew what it was like to be in a hospital, I asked to be allowed to help Al and his family.

My first meeting with Al was on the afternoon of 9/11 when I went up to the ICU at the Jersey City Medical Center. A few other people had been brought over from the World Trade Center, but Al had the most severe, possibly fatal injuries. I had gone up to the side of Al's bed, thinking he was unconscious, when all of a sudden he grabbed my hand. He scared me. He had tubes down his throat, but he was trying to talk. I eventually made out what he was saying. "How many brothers?" he kept asking, in a muffled, gasping voice.

I did not know who Al was, but those were the first words I heard him say. I was amazed that he had gone through all he had and was asking, "How many brothers?" I told him, "Don't worry about it. We're working on getting everybody out." Then he passed out.

That night I came back to check on the rest of those who had been brought in from New York City. I eventually acted as a liaison between Jersey City and the F.D.N.Y. I faxed over, on the night of 9/11, a list to New York City as to who was in the hospital. Many of those who were first brought in, were transferred out in the next day or two, but Al was too sick to be moved.

We took over the doctors' conference room down the hall with beverages that the hospital provided, at first. The hospital was tremendous in supplying whatever we needed with cases of water, sandwiches, or ice. Tom Murphy, Director of the Jersey City Office of Emergency Management said, "Mike, try and go out and get some of the restaurants to help."

I got a couple. One was Puccini's Restaurant, owned by Pasquale Puccini. He's a good man. Pasquale brought over the food himself from his restaurant, which is a fine restaurant in Jersey City. Most of the time, I would meet him in front of the emergency room. Every day he would bring this huge food warmer and trays of food filled with steaks, macaroni, and chicken. I've told people, "On 9/11, we saw the best of people at the worst of times," and Pasquale was one of these.

He told me, "I came here from Italy and I had no money. I started a restaurant. I'm doing well and I want to give back. I want to give back." He is a man who really cares from the heart, which makes him similar to firefighters who give of themselves, each day.

In addition to Puccini's, other places helped out. I think the VIP Diner on the Boulevard provided breakfast, so that we now had the doctors' conference room filled with trays of donated food being brought in from the local restaurants. Every person wanted to help. So many people showed up to do what they could.

Eileen, Mike and Lorraine were there all the time. I met Al's mom and dad, as well as his sisters and brother. What a great family. They seemed to be a typical fire department family, real tight knit and ready to help each other. Eileen is an unbelievable woman. She was strong, and could have run the whole scene. She cried a little – so did a lot of firefighters who went up there – but she kept control.

It was a big chore keeping away people and the media from trying to see Al. When I screened people, I'd say, "It's the family's wishes not to have visitors now." Some firefighters from Jersey City came by to bring something and to briefly stop by to see Al, but we limited visits because he was so ill.

THE TRIP BACK TO NEW YORK CITY

It was a tremendous experience bringing Al over in the ambulance. I was in a marked Jersey City Fire Department car, and we came down Montgomery Street in Jersey City. When we got to the Lincoln Tunnel, two State Police Highway Patrol cars, a Port Authority car, and a police car joined our entourage.

As we drove along West Street, people were standing along the side of the road and holding up little signs they had made that read, "We love you. We love the FDNY and the NYPD." The people knew somebody was being transported and the support was fantastic. I saw hundreds of people cheering and waving flags as we drove by. It was such a stirring sight of support. It brought tears to my eyes to see so much love being shown Al and us. I don't know if I'll ever see that again in my lifetime.

As we drove through the city, more and more marked and unmarked police cars joined in. They had their lights flashing and kept getting in front to make sure that we kept moving. We drove from midtown up to Montefiore Hopital in the Bronx. When we arrived there, we made sure Al got to his room, and then we hung out for a while.

Here again, everyone was so great about wanting to help. Again, the restaurants provided food, with Starbucks generously sending over coffee and muffins.

THE REUNION MORE THAN A YEAR LATER

More than a year later, I was with Al and Eileen, after they gave the Jersey City Fire Department a plaque for their help, and we went to Pasquale's restaurant for dinner. That's when we bumped into the nurses from the ICU. Talk about fate. Everybody was happy and crying. It was a great reunion. The ICU staff at the Jersey City Medical Center does an excellent job.

Al's a tough guy. As sick as he was, that first day he grabbed my hand he was as strong as a bull. I was touched that he was so concerned for all the other brothers. That showed what kind of character he has. He's a good, good man.

I only met Al during his stay at the hospital, but I feel very close to him, his family, his friends, and the FDNY brothers. He left a mark on my life. In the fire department, we take care of our own. We're a family to each other. I am honored to have been able to help Al, a brother firefighter.

September 11th, 2001

after you get beyond
wondering where he was
when the first plane hit
standing at the water-cooler or
ribbing a co-worker at his desk, or
crouching and twisting
a wire into light, or gazing
out one of those windows
into what we thought were
the heavens, remembering a kiss
or the milk he had to pick up
on the way home that night,
after you close your eyes
in the dark womb
of that truck, to his fixed only on the fire up ahead
after you get beyond asking
was she on a staircase with others
too much a part of what was happening
to taste her own fear, was the comfort
of being and doing enough, was there calm
and not the thought of what was
to be, on those stairs
when you can let your mind
let go of the children
they became, let go of
your own devouring longing
to hold them in your arms and
carry them down
when you can let that be
and those we've seen so many times
make their way up there
to that moment they all met
and Life was still a possibility
of such enormous bearing, stop
frame that picture, and
hang it in the dim and sacred
gallery of your mind
set a candle before it
to burn in the night
do not look away, but see
how they held one another, held each of us
(the way we hold each other now)
rising, rising, rising
as the world around them shuddered

Helen Morrissey Rizzuto